SEARCH N
RESCUE

SEARCH N
RESCUE

EDDIE ROMAN

BRIDGE
LOGOS

Newberry, FL 32669

Bridge-Logos
Newberry, FL 32669

Search N Rescue
Guiding Unbelievers To The Savior
by Eddie Roman

Printed in the United States of America

Library of Congress Catalog Card Number: 2018949493

International Standard Book Number: 9781610362160

Edited by Lynn Copeland

Scripture quotations taken from the New American Standard Bible® (NASB). Copyright © 1960, 1962, 1963, 1968, 1971, 1972, 1973, 1975, 1977, 1995 by The Lockman Foundation. Used by permission. www.Lockman.org.

For more resources from Eddie Roman, visit eddieroman.com

Cover/Interior design by Kent Jensen | knail.com

To Carri,
the love of my life

◇◇◇◇◇◇◇◇◇◇◇◇◇◇◇◇◇◇◇◇◇◇◇◇◇◇◇◇◇◇◇◇

"For the Son of Man has come to seek
and to save that which was lost."

—Luke 19:10

◇◇◇◇◇◇◇◇◇◇◇◇◇◇◇◇◇◇◇◇◇◇◇◇◇◇◇◇◇◇◇◇

CONTENTS

FOREWORD

Eddie Roman is the brilliant producer and director of our award-winning television program. I'm honored to, not only count him as a good friend, but say that he's a true faithful witness of Jesus Christ. Like the Apostle Paul, Eddie's not ashamed of the gospel. He loves God and he loves people—and that love is clearly evident by his on-going evangelistic lifestyle. He ignores his fears and regularly shares the gospel on a one to one basis, and he regularly stands up in the open air and *preaches* the gospel in a loving way that engages the lost.

My sincere hope and prayer is that you not only read this wonderful book, but that you put its biblical principles into practice.

—Ray Comfort

INTRODUCTION

If you are a Christian, you understand the biblical message of the gospel. You know that all men and women are sinners, deserving of God's wrath. You agree with Scripture that mankind stands guilty before God and that every guilty person deserves to spend eternity in hell. If you are a Christian, you also know that Jesus Christ came to save sinners. He saved you from the terrible punishment you deserve, and for that, you are eternally grateful. It is only natural that you would want to take this great salvation message and share it with everyone around you. My hope is that God would use this book to help you do just that.

For many Christians, evangelism is something reserved for mission trips or when a sermon forces us to think about the unbelievers we know. Whatever the reason, most believers do not view evangelism as a regular part of the Christian experience. The purpose of this book is to change that. God can make evangelism a natural part of your Christian life, just as normal as prayer, reading your Bible, and attending church services. As with prayer, Bible study, and church involvement, evangelism begins with the desire to do it. Scripture is clear that God wants His children to spread the good news of everlasting life, and He has provided us with all the knowledge and power to do so.

Search N Rescue is a mixture of Scripture and practical instruction. Naturally, the Bible has much to say about evangelism;

it is our ultimate authority on why and how we should evangelize. The practical guidance in this book comes from years of street evangelism, which is simply sharing the gospel with strangers you encounter in public—the way the disciples did. I'll relate some of my witnessing experiences—the good, the bad, and the funny. Yes, funny. I have been street witnessing and open-air preaching for over five years, and trust me, weird stuff happens when you stand on a box and preach the gospel in public. I'll be the first to admit it's not exactly normal (though it's very biblical). While I do not believe every Christian should be an open-air preacher, I will say that street evangelism has taught me many valuable lessons about people, myself, and how to share the gospel.

I used to think evangelism was difficult and scary, but things have changed. I love talking to unbelievers about Jesus Christ, and it's not because I tiptoe around hard issues. I tell them about sin, hell, judgment, the fact that homosexuality is wrong, and every other politically incorrect issue that comes up. I also tell them about the Savior. I rarely have anger or hatred directed at me, and when I do, God gets me through it.

I love evangelism; it's brought me joy, excitement, fun, fulfillment, great new friends, and a deeper level of intimacy with and dependence on Christ. Sure, it has brought trials as well, but so does everything else in life that's worth doing. Any inconvenience or persecution you will ever face will pale in comparison to the joy of knowing you are being employed by God to save men and women from an eternal hell. The things of this world are passing, but in six million years, when you look around heaven and see people you once preached the gospel to... wow. My friend, don't let anything hold you back. Preach the gospel! Make yourself ready and available to be used by God in the saving of souls.

This book can be used for individual study or within the context of an evangelism class or other group study. Questions at the end of each chapter are designed to help you identify things in your life that may be hindering your evangelism effort. Please take the time to watch the suggested online videos as well, as they are meant to encourage you. Finally, the prayer point at the end of each chapter will help keep you focused on Jesus Christ, the Master Evangelist.

I hope you will see this book as something to guide your evangelism efforts as you read, rather than a book you have to finish before you begin evangelizing. Evangelism is a spiritual discipline, as is prayer. You might not think you are praying in the best way possible, but I would never tell a Christian to read a book on prayer before they begin praying. Books on prayer and evangelism can help us to do the activity better, but we should never think of them as required reading before participating in things that God has commanded us to do. If you're not aware that God has commanded us to evangelize, hopefully this book will help you to understand that...and to joyfully obey.

THE GIRL WHO SHUT ME UP

Huntington Beach, California, is a hot spot for evangelism. Christians of all kinds go there with a Bible in hand and a pocketful of gospel tracts, hoping to lead unbelievers to Christ. I had been going weekly one summer, tagging along with a group of street evangelists. It was intimidating at first, giving gospel tracts to strangers. Some would take it; others wouldn't. As a literature distributor, I seldom spoke with the people I handed tracts to—but it was better that way since I didn't know what to say. I left the witnessing conversations to the veteran Christians. However, most of the conversation took place among us Christians. It was a fun time; we would come up with cheesy opening lines to use as we handed out tracts. No serious hellfire types here, just a bunch of laid-back Californians sharing Jesus on a Friday night. Our group of twenty-somethings was more silly than serious.

Rave Girl Strikes

A couple of months into my evangelism venture, I had a new one-liner that needed to be released. Rave clubs were in abundance, and I spotted a group of dance/drug types hanging out on the corner, ready to party. So I grabbed a stack of postcard-sized tracts that looked like Rave invites and walked over to the group announcing, "Party! Party! Free party in heaven!" Well, it made my friend laugh, but it did not have the same effect on the group. One of the girls took the tract and read it, then began yelling at me. "You liar—this isn't a party, it's a stupid church thing! You're lying! You're a liar!"

I learned two valuable lessons that day. First, I found out that unbelievers do not laugh at the same cheesy jokes believers might laugh at. (Many people do not laugh at dumb jokes at all, but that's beside the point.) Second, I learned that I'm not as thick-skinned as I thought, because that teenage girl's anger was all it took to stop my evangelism efforts cold. I went home that night with a head full of questions, doubts, fear, and a clear revelation that some people hate you for reaching out to them. Believe it or not, this small rebuke was enough to cripple my evangelism for years.

As time moved on, I became a small-group Bible study leader and then got involved with disaster relief missions. Eventually, I was on staff at a church with a strong disaster relief focus, and I spent my days traveling in and out of Africa on short-term mission trips. Like many mission trips that originate from American churches, we spent a lot of time doing works of compassion (which are important and good), but very little time sharing the gospel with unbelievers. I was a missionary who didn't preach the gospel much, if at all. Once I had the opportunity to preach to a huge crowd through a translator after we played the *JESUS* film, and I'm pretty sure I explained the gospel clearly, but I don't remember explaining the gospel to an unbeliever at any other time during my years working in Africa. But I didn't lose much sleep over it; I had found my place within the body of Christ and church activities became my life. I was busy with Bible study groups, prayer meetings, church, church, and more church. I loved it because I love Jesus. So life continued and all was well—except for evangelism. As much as I knew I should, I just couldn't get the gospel out of my mouth. When I was with unbelievers, I would make small talk, but somehow I always managed to avoid talking about Christ, heaven, and hell. If you're a Christian with a basic understanding of Scripture, you know that hell is real and that unbelievers are going there for all eternity, including some of the people you know. Hopefully, you're not okay with that, so it's something we need to warn people about.

Fear of Man

I eventually realized that I wouldn't talk about Christ because I lived in bondage to the fear of man. The Bible tells us, *"The fear of man brings a snare, but he who trusts in the LORD will be exalted"* (Proverbs 29:25). It would take years for me to focus on the second half of that verse because the fear of man was a huge snare for me. It wasn't so much that I was afraid of people; I just feared their reaction to the gospel. I didn't want to be looked down on or ridiculed or despised. I like fun and friends, and I wanted none of this conflict stuff. Being around church friends was so much easier than being around unbelievers. They didn't cuss, listen to gangster rap, view pornography, or any of the other things I had stopped doing and was trying to avoid. I never thought I was better than my unbelieving friends; I just stopped enjoying the same things we used to talk about.

As God was changing me day by day, I began to hate sin and love righteousness. My interests were different, and I had no desire to live my old life. I continued to give my time to the pursuit of God within the community of His people, the church. I knew as a Christian I was supposed to evangelize, but... "whatever." It was much easier not to.

Looking back to that night at Huntington Beach and the years of complacency that followed, I stand amazed at how far the Lord has brought me. Today I go out of my way to talk to strangers about Jesus Christ. By God's grace, I lead the evangelism ministry at my church, and I work full-time for a ministry that teaches people how to evangelize. I have debated atheists on the campus of UC Berkeley and other universities. I have stood on a soapbox and preached the gospel in secular settings to thousands of people. That scared young man who dropped his tracts and ran away from the teenage girl is long gone. Why? Simply because God can do exceedingly abundantly beyond all we can ask for or think (Ephesians 3:20).

God changed me, and He can change you. If you have a desire to evangelize, but you cannot bring yourself to share the gospel, this book is for you. I am going to show you what God did in my life as well as what He can do in your life to make you into someone who is not afraid to share the gospel. Though your story is not the same as mine, if you're a Christian, your God is the same as mine, and He can make you a soul winner, a fisher of men. The words Jesus spoke to His first followers are just as relevant to us today: *"Follow Me, and I will make you fishers of men"* (Matthew 4:19).

///

If you have a desire to evangelize, but you cannot bring yourself to share the gospel, this book is for you

\\\

My goal in these pages is to help you learn to share the gospel of Jesus Christ. We will look at what the Bible says about the gospel message, evangelism, and our involvement in reaching the lost. The purpose of this book is not to make you into a street preacher or a door-to-door evangelist. God might not want to use you in those areas, but if God does want to use you for evangelism in any capacity (and I have a strong hunch He does), then you need to be ready.

Who Should Evangelize?

For years I served in ministry, yet I was unwilling to share my faith with the unbelievers around me. I knew I should reach out, but I didn't. Instead I pushed it aside because that was easier. If you had asked me about my walk with the Lord, I would have said, "Yeah, I'm doing good, not perfect, but good." I was raised Catholic, and part of the Catholic mentality is the idea that priests, nuns, the Pope, and "professional holy people" are the ones who do the spiritual work; laymen don't need to. Some of that mentality stuck with me in the early days of my Christian life.

I did not understand the biblical concept of the priesthood of all believers. Every believer should obey and serve Christ in all areas, and this would include the often-neglected area of evangelism.

Jesus was not speaking to church leaders in Matthew 28, but to anyone who would follow Him: *"Go therefore and make disciples of all the nations, baptizing them in the name of the Father and the Son and the Holy Spirit"* (Matthew 28:19). This verse is known as the "Great Commission." It is a call to all believers to make disciples, which begins with explaining the gospel and inviting a person to follow Christ. Christian, you are inside the church. Unbelievers are outside of the church. To make disciples, you need to go outside of the church building and evangelize the unbelievers, then bring them into the church and disciple them. Discipleship takes many forms, but it always begins with someone sharing the gospel. This is normal Christianity— believers engaged in reaching lost souls for Christ. We see this right from the beginning of the church:

> *"But you will receive power when the Holy Spirit has come upon you; and you shall be My witnesses both in Jerusalem, and in all Judea and Samaria, and even to the remotest part of the earth"* (Acts 1:8)

> *"And every day, in the temple and from house to house, they kept right on teaching and preaching Jesus as the Christ"* (Acts 5:42)

> *"Therefore, those who had been scattered went about preaching the word"* (Acts 8:4)

When persecution hit the church in Jerusalem, all the Christians were scattered to other areas, and everyone preached about Jesus as they went. The believers communicated the gospel with the people around them, as did the leaders of the church. Paul spent his life for the gospel. Everywhere he went, Paul talked to people about Jesus and their need for salvation; he *"kept declaring both to those of Damascus first, and also at Jerusalem and then throughout all the region of Judea, and even to the Gentiles, that they should repent and turn to God, performing deeds appropriate to repentance"* (Acts 26:20). He confirmed to the church elders, *"I did not shrink from declaring to you anything that was profitable, and teaching you publicly and from house to house, solemnly testifying to both Jews and Greeks of repentance toward God and faith in our Lord Jesus Christ"* (Acts 20:20,21).

Men and women who love God must be willing to be used by Him for anything, including sharing the gospel. *"For I am not ashamed of the gospel, for it is the power of God for salvation to everyone who believes, to the Jew first and also to the Greek"* (Romans 1:16). Is this verse true of you? We should never be ashamed of the gospel—the power of God.

It is an honor to be used by God, the King of all creation. God is the one who saves, but He graciously involves Christians in the process of salvation. God wants to use us to preach the gospel message to the lost: *"How then will they call on Him in whom they have not believed? How will they believe in Him whom they have not heard? And how will they hear without a preacher?"* (Romans 10:14). God saved us for His purpose, and part of His mission includes our participation in the reconciliation of the lost. We are His agents, His ambassadors of reconciliation. Let these words sink in:

> Now all these things are from God, who reconciled us to Himself through Christ and gave us the ministry of reconciliation, namely, that God was in Christ reconciling the world to Himself, not counting their trespasses against them, and He has committed to us the word of reconciliation. Therefore, we are ambassadors for Christ, as though God were making an appeal through us; we beg you on behalf of Christ, be reconciled to God.　　　　　　　　　　　(2 Corinthians 5:18–20)

While I do not believe every Christian has to open-air preach or evangelize on the streets, every Christian should be available for God's use as a minister of reconciliation. For some, it will be to their coworkers or neighbors. For others, perhaps it will be the parents in their PTA group or at sports events. Where and how God uses you is not the issue; your willingness to be used by Him is what matters.

The Gift of Evangelism

What if you don't have the "gift of evangelism"? Doesn't that make you exempt from having to talk to all those lost people? Some people claim that Ephesians 4 gives the average Christian a pass on witnessing, since the job of preaching the gospel is only for those with the gift. Let's examine that. Speaking of the gifts God gave to the church, Paul says, *"And He gave some as apostles, and some as prophets, and some as evangelists, and some as pastors and teachers, for the equipping of the saints for the work of service, to the building up of the body of Christ"* (Ephesians 4:11,12).

As always, it's good to read things in context. It is clear that God has given some believers the role of the evangelist, but we need to keep reading to find out the purpose of that role. In verse 12 we are told the evangelist is for *"the equipping of the saints for the work of service, to the building up of the body of Christ"* (Ephesians 4:12). God has gifted some people the evangelism in order to equip, teach, and encourage His church to evangelize! Have you ever heard an evangelist teach and tell stories of how God has miraculously saved people? Have you ever been encouraged or equipped by an evangelist? If so, you have benefited from the gift of evangelism in the way God intended. The role of the gifted evangelist is to equip you, the Christian, to do the work of evangelism.

In the same way, God has called certain people to be pastors and teachers. We would never say, "I'm not going to teach my kids the Bible, because I don't have the gift of teaching." We understand that pastors teach us, and then we take those truths and teach them to our kids. I personally do not have the gift of giving. Should I not tithe? That would be a bad excuse. The gifts are meant to benefit the body of Christ in specific ways, but we should never use our lack of a certain gift as an excuse to exempt ourselves from service. Praise the Lord for the gifts He has given us. We need gifted pastors, teachers, and evangelists.

Dealing With Fear

Most Christians understand we are supposed to share the gospel with unbelievers. Years after my encounter with Rave Girl, as I coasted through my un-evangelistic Evangelical Christian life, had you asked me if we should evangelize, my answer would have been yes. If your next question had to do with the last time I evangelized, I would have laughed or sighed, depending on what kind of mood I was in. We know we should be about our Father's business, but fear hinders many of us. As mentioned earlier, *"The fear of man brings a snare..."* (Proverbs 29:25). Think of that: "the fear of man." How do we fear people? We fear they might disagree with us. We fear the teasing and the possibility that they will think we are stupid, uneducated, unscientific, or illogical because of our "childish" belief in God. In some cases, we fear physical intimidation or violence against us.

I have a friend whose Jewish dad is a former Golden Gloves boxing champion. My friend shared the gospel with him at a family function, and his father punched him in the face. His own dad tried to knock him out! Fortunately, my friend is a martial arts expert, so he survived, but can you imagine? Most of us will never be punched in the face by a loved one, but we fear being punched emotionally. Our desire to fit in with our unbelieving friends and to be accepted by coworkers and family keeps the fear of rejection high.

So how can we get past the fear of man? What can we do to place God and the gospel above our fears? Let's look again at Proverbs 29:25: *"The fear of man brings a snare, but he who trusts in the LORD will be exalted."* The second half of the verse is the answer: trust in the Lord. This is a common theme throughout the Bible. For example, God assured Joshua, *"Have I not commanded you? Be strong and courageous! Do not tremble or be dismayed, for the LORD your God is with you wherever you go"* (Joshua 1:9). The simple truth that God is always with you should be a tremendous comfort, a reason to press on and do whatever you know God wants you to do at any given moment. God is all-powerful, and He's with us when we evangelize to give us strength and courage. This is a truth that we often overlook. Cling to the Lord; He will help you overcome fear.

The opposite of fear is faith. In allowing our fears to regulate our actions, we miss the joy of living by faith in a God who blesses His children by using them in the process of saving souls. God wants us to trust Him. When we go against our emotions and step out in the area of evangelism, God is pleased. *"And without faith, it is impossible to please Him, for he who comes to God must believe that He is and that He is a rewarder of those who seek Him"* (Hebrews 11:6). Evangelism requires faith in God.

One of the most rewarding experiences of the Christian life is to be used in the salvation of a soul. One night I was with my sons at a huge Christmas event in Riverside, California, where thousands of people had come to see a Christmas lights display at the Mission Inn Hotel. I was doing "sketchboard" evangelism, a technique popularized by the ministry Open Air Campaigners. It involves attracting attention in a crowded area by painting with glow-in-the-dark paint. People will gather around you to watch you paint. At some point you turn to the crowd and explain what you are painting, then you begin telling a story as you paint your way through a (soon to be revealed) gospel message. The presentation takes fifteen to thirty minutes, depending on crowd interaction. That night, after the message, the crowd dispersed except for one young woman, around age twenty-five. She slowly walked up to talk to me. She had been listening to the entire gospel presentation and said, "I want to be forgiven by God." To say it made me happy would be an understatement. I spoke with her for a while, making sure she understood salvation, repentance, and faith. With tears, she prayed for God's forgiveness and put her trust in Christ. It was beautiful, watching someone pray to trust Christ right there on a city sidewalk. I love evangelism!

One of the most rewarding
experiences of the Christian life is to
be used in the salvation of a soul.

Fear of Man, or Fear for Man?

Instead of fearing man, we should fear *for* man. We should be fearful of the fate of any who remain in sin, lost without Christ. Our attitude toward unbelievers should not be to fear them, but to be concerned for them. Five hundred years from now, acceptance of our peers and invitations to family gatherings are not going to matter. Heaven and hell will matter. Let's replace our fear of man with fear for man, keeping in mind that *"it is a terrifying thing to fall into the hands of the living God"* (Hebrews 10:31). My martial arts friend knew his Golden Gloves dad wasn't going to like hearing about Jesus. His attempt to share Christ regardless of the outcome revealed his compassion was greater than his fear of man.

In light of who God is, there is no reason to fear any man. Think of the most hateful enemy of Christ, maybe a member of ISIS, someone who has no problem killing Christians for preaching the gospel. Then consider this verse: *"Do not fear those who kill the body but are unable to kill the soul; but rather fear Him who is able to destroy both soul and body in hell"* (Matthew 10:28). Do you believe in hell? Jesus does. Hell is a very real place, and unbelievers are going there.

Matthew 25 contains the parable of the sheep and the goats. At the end of the parable, Jesus gives a summary of the fates of unbelievers and believers. It's among the most joyful as well as the most horrific verses in the Bible. Speaking of unbelievers (the goats) Jesus says, *"These will go away into eternal punishment, but the righteous into eternal life"* (Matthew 25:46). "The righteous" (the sheep) refers to those who have trusted in the righteousness of Christ. This verse shows something very sobering. It indicates that death is final and there are only two places people go when they die—either heaven or hell. There is no purgatory, nirvana, reincarnation, nothingness, or anything else. It's either heaven or hell, for all of eternity.

Heaven or Hell?

Put aside all your deep theological knowledge for a moment, all the things you've learned over years of Bible study concerning eschatology, the Trinity, the hypostatic union, the believer's role in government, and all the things that new believers don't quite grasp at first. One of the most basic concepts of Christianity is this: every man, woman, and child ever born will go to either heaven or hell. We don't think twice about believing in heaven, but hell is a difficult concept for some who do not understand the extent of God's holiness and man's sinfulness. If you don't think mankind deserves hell, it may be because you don't understand how holy and righteous God is, and how wicked and sinful man is. God is too holy to allow sin in His presence: *"Your eyes are too pure to approve evil, and You can not look on wickedness with favor"* (Habakkuk 1:13). Speaking of God, Psalm 5:4 adds, "No evil dwells with You.

///

One of the most basic concepts
of Christianity is this: every man,
woman, and child ever born will go to
either heaven or hell.

\\

Hell is God's place of punishment for sin. We will look at the sinful nature of man in the next chapter. For now, it's important to realize what's at stake in salvation. Without Christ, the problem is not that people are lacking happiness or fulfillment in life. They are headed for hell, *forever.* Not a pretty thought, but that's precisely the point. It's a horrible future, and that's exactly why they need a Savior. God has chosen us, His people, as the messengers of His glorious gospel. We need to have a realistic view of heaven and hell. Our apprehension to witness may be real, but in light of eternity, it is unreasonable for us to allow the fear of man to hinder our attempts to reach the lost.

Emergency Mode

During my silent years, I did manage to squeak the gospel out once in a while, when it was (in my opinion) an "emergency." I was working on a BMX video in Tuscaloosa, Alabama, and a rider asked if I would go with him to visit his dying father in the hospital. The man was in bed, unable to speak, riddled with cancer. I was looking at someone who was days away from eternity. I stepped out of my comfort zone and explained the gospel to him. He could not speak, so I asked him to squeeze my hand if he wanted to trust in Christ. He squeezed, and three days later he was dead.

Things like this happened occasionally. I would find myself in an "emergency" situation where someone was at death's door, and I would be compelled to share the gospel. Over a period of ten years, I may have explained the gospel to an unbeliever four or five times. My perspective, of course, was wrong. The thought that certain situations are "emergencies" and that during "normal life" there is no need to preach the gospel is just wrong logically as well as biblically. Logically it makes no sense since I have no idea when anyone is going to die. Scripture tells us, *"Yet you do not know what your life will be like tomorrow. You are just a vapor that appears for a little while and then vanishes away"* (James 4:14). The idea that it's okay to preach the gospel only when it's urgent is unbiblical. The Bible instructs us to preach the gospel in any given situation, not just when we deem it necessary.

So what changed me? How did I go from coward to open-air preacher? To begin with, I went through a year of conviction. More than fifteen years into my Christian life of complacency, out of nowhere, I felt convicted about my lack of evangelism. That persisted for about a year. I wanted so badly to talk to the lost about Jesus, but I couldn't bring myself to do it. It was torture, wanting to do the right thing but not knowing what to say. Fearful of how people might respond, I was just plain disobedient to the Scriptures. I knew what the Bible said; I'd heard the call to evangelize at church repeatedly, and I even wanted to, but I was scared. Then one day I was surfing the web and came across Ray Comfort, an evangelist who often videotapes his personal witnessing encounters. I watched many of his videos and eventually came across an ad for his "Ambassadors' Academy," a three-day evangelism seminar in Southern California. They did crazy stuff at this workshop, like open-air preaching on Hollywood Boulevard and Huntington Beach. Under normal circumstances, I might have passed it by, but with the Holy Spirit's conviction heavy on my heart, I considered the seminar and came to the conclusion that it might just help. So I signed up. God used that weekend to change the direction of my life.

The Big Change

The Ambassadors' Academy was a whirlwind of teaching, witnessing, and open-air preaching. Many things happened, but the main thing for me occurred before the evangelism even started. We were riding in a tour bus on the way to Hollywood. In a short time, I would be standing on a stepstool (street preachers call it "the box") and preaching the gospel to (at least in my mind) thousands of God-hating tourists. Looking out the bus window, thoughts and emotions raced through my mind. I couldn't believe what was about to happen. Here I was, the shy guy, the guy who never talks about God in public, the guy who was raised in a very non-confrontational home with parents who never argued! In my over-exaggerated imagination, passive little me was about to step into a hornet's nest of angry atheists, militant homosexuals, Muslim extremists, and every other hater of Christianity.

I had so many reasons why I couldn't open my mouth over the years since I'd become a Christian, so many excuses. A thought came to mind during my ride to Hollywood, and that was...*I'm sorry.* I'm sorry for disobeying God. I'm sorry that I've suppressed the truth for so long. I had been disobedient; I knew I should evangelize, but for over fifteen years as a Christian, I did not. I confessed my sin of disobedience to God, and right there on that bus in the midst of LA traffic, I repented. I asked God to forgive me.

The Bible is clear that disobedience is sin. Consider these words of Jesus:

"Why do you call Me, 'Lord, Lord,' and do not do what I say?"
(Luke 6:46)

"Not everyone who says to Me, 'Lord, Lord,' will enter the kingdom of heaven, but he who does the will of My Father who is in heaven will enter" (Matthew 7:21)

"He who has My commandments and keeps them is the one who loves Me; and he who loves Me will be loved by My Father, and I will love him and will disclose Myself to him" (John 14:21)

For years I had denied the obvious. I was being disobedient because I was afraid to evangelize.

I had rationalized it away whenever necessary, but on that bus, I admitted my sin and God forgave me. He forgave me for my fear of man and my disobedience. If that had been the extent of my experience at the seminar, it would have been more than worth it. Fortunately for me, my weekend had just begun. With the guilt and shame of disobedience behind me, I stepped off the bus with joy. My team leader placed the box on the sidewalk in a busy section of Hollywood Boulevard. I watched in amazement as veteran street evangelists took turns getting on the box, preaching mini-sermons to curious tourists and getting into apologetic debates with enemies of Christ. It was wild to watch, and before I knew it, my team leader was telling me it was my turn. Without hesitation, I got on the box, and it was totally freeing. *"So if the Son makes you free, you will be free indeed"* (John 8:36). I had been a slave to my sinful fear of man and my sin of disobedience. Following Christ is freeing!

Repent

Have you been disobeying God's command to evangelize? Do you live in fear of man, afraid to open your mouth and speak the truth to the unbelievers in your life? If so, your emotions and reasoning may be complex, but the answer is simple. You need to repent. God's Word assures us, *"If we confess our sins, He is faithful and righteous to forgive us our sins and to cleanse us from all unrighteousness"* (1 John 1:9). Ask God to forgive you for fearing man more than Him. Ask Him to forgive you for disobeying Him in the area of evangelism. He will forgive you. Then ask Him for the strength to do His will.

Many churches and evangelism ministries have convinced us that their book, their method, or their philosophy is what we need to become good at evangelism. Others attempt to fill you with apologetic answers to prepare you for the objections that will come your way. All these things can be helpful, but nothing will get you out of the church and into the world to reach the lost if you are unwilling to open your mouth and talk about the gospel with unbelievers. If you have given in to fear, repent. Maybe there is something else you need to repent of such as complacency, anger toward the lost (like Jonah), or self-righteousness ("they deserve to go to hell, unlike me"). Whatever the case, pray to God, asking Him to reveal your reason for disobedience.

Maybe you did not realize you are supposed to be evangelizing. Sadly, many churches are so self-focused that they rarely, if ever, think about the lost. Once a year they have a missionary come in and tell tales of what it's like to talk to lost people on the other side of the world. Once a year! A church environment like that will not instill in you a heart for evangelism.

Many Christians do not evangelize because they have never been taught. Some churches have an "evangelism expert" on staff, and they tell members to bring their unsaved friends to church services so they can hear the gospel from the expert. In a church setting like that, it's easy to be mistaken that evangelism is only for the "gifted," not the average church attendee. Whatever the case, it's time to start following Christ, the One who came to seek and save the lost.

God Sends Us on Mission

Do you know why Jesus came to earth? He did many things while He walked the roads of Israel, but His primary purpose was very clear. Christ came to save sinners:

> *"She will bear a Son; and you shall call His name Jesus, for He will save His people from their sins"* (Matthew 1:21)

> *"For the Son of Man has come to seek and to save that which was lost"* (Luke 19:10)

"It is a trustworthy statement, deserving full acceptance, that Christ Jesus came into the world to save sinners, among whom I am foremost of all" (1 Timothy 1:15)

Sometimes we have to search to try to understand God's will for our life in a particular area. This is not necessary with evangelism, because we know God wants to save sinners and we know He wants all believers to evangelize.

So often we choose to trust God with our family, our job, and every other area of life. Why don't we trust Him with evangelism? He obviously wants to save sinners. Ultimately, God is the one who evangelizes and saves people; we are just His messengers. This is an important concept to understand. Jesus is the great evangelist who draws people to Himself. *"And I, if I am lifted up from the earth, will draw all men to Myself"* (John 12:32). Our job is simple. We lift up the name of Jesus, and He does the drawing of people to Himself. God is so much more concerned about the lost than we are, and His love for them is far greater than ours will ever be. That's why John 3:16 is such a powerfully comforting verse: *"For God so loved the world, that He gave His only begotten Son, that whoever believes in Him shall not perish, but have eternal life."*

The fact that God loves and draws sinners to Himself should be an encouragement to us as we seek His help in sharing the gospel. God is on a mission and He has chosen to take us along with Him to reach the lost. Just as Jesus was sent into the world to save sinners, Jesus tells His followers, *"As the Father has sent Me, I also send you"* (John 20:21). Some people go on mission trips once in a while, and that's a good thing. But if we are willing, God can make our entire life a thrilling mission trip as we serve Him by evangelizing the lost wherever we go.

Are you ready to be His messenger? I hope so! In the next chapter, we'll look at the message God has given us to share.

QUESTIONS FOR REFLECTION /////////////////////////////

1. Eddie's first roadblock in evangelism was Rave Girl. Have you ever had a difficult experience that discouraged your evangelism efforts? If you are reading this book with a group, share your experiences.

2. What are some of the reasons you have used to not evangelize? Based on this chapter, are any of them valid excuses? Explain.

3. According to Matthew 4:19, if we are truly followers of Christ, what will we become?

4. Who should be evangelizing, and why?

5. How would you explain the "gift" of evangelism?

6. What are some ways we can get past our fears of witnessing?

7. If you have been disobedient toward God and His command to evangelize, what should you do about that? Will you do that now? _____

_____

_____

_____

8. Explain whether you believe God is powerful and good enough to help you as you step out in faith to preach the gospel to the lost. _____

_____

_____

_____

WATCH THIS! ///

- Time for a break! Go to eddieroman.com and click Watch on the top menu.
- Watch the video labeled "Don't Be Afraid." Can you relate?

PRAYER POINT ///

- Ask God to help you get past your fears and reach out to the lost.

2

WHAT THE GOSPEL IS AND ISN'T

"There's a knife in my back; I have three minutes to live. Can you tell me how to get to heaven?" This question, originated by evangelist Ray Comfort, is a quick way to find out what someone believes about the afterlife. It's also a great test for Christians. Can you explain the gospel message in three minutes? How about two? One? The apostle Paul could do it in about ten seconds: *"For I delivered to you as of first importance what I also received, that Christ died for our sins according to the Scriptures, and that He was buried, and that He was raised on the third day according to the Scriptures"* (1 Corinthians 15:3,4).

I think 1 Corinthians 15:3,4 is the clearest, most concise explanation of the gospel in the Bible. What is the gospel? It's that Jesus Christ died for our sins and rose again. This is so important to remember in a day when people tend to make up own their definitions. People use terms like "gospel truth" and "gospel music." Mormons claim to teach the gospel, and Catholics read from the gospel. The term "gospel" can mean different things to different people, but as far as the Bible is concerned, the gospel is the good news of the death and resurrection of Jesus Christ. So with that in mind, here's a question. If a gospel singer is singing a Christian song that does not mention the death and resurrection of Jesus Christ, are they singing gospel music? In a biblical sense, I'd say no. It might be a great song, and it might be part of the style of music we've come to know as "gospel," but if there's no death and resurrection of Jesus, there's no gospel in the gospel music. Fortunately for the gospel music industry, my technical definition doesn't matter, and we all understand what gospel music is. It's part of church culture.

Let's look at another "gospel" part of church culture—an invitation that includes a "sinner's prayer." Maybe you have been at an evangelistic church service or outreach where you heard the speaker say something like this: "If there's anyone here who would like to accept Jesus Christ into their heart, just raise your hand. If you want Christ to fill the void in your life, I'm going to ask you to pray with me in a minute. Jesus loves you. He can fulfill your needs; He can make your life better and make you new. If you want to get right with God and go to heaven when you die, pray this prayer with me. 'Dear God, I know I'm a sinner. I ask you to forgive me of my sin. Please come into my heart and make me new. I accept you as my Savior. Thank you so much. Amen.'"

Many of us have heard and even responded to similar words coming from the pulpit. Now here's the big question: What's wrong with that gospel presentation? The most obvious problem is, it doesn't have the gospel in it. No mention of the death and resurrection of Jesus Christ. This is known as an epic fail. Sadly, this doesn't just come from the pulpit.

I often meet Christians while I'm out witnessing, and on occasion I'll say to them, "There's a knife in my back, and I have three minutes to live. Tell me how to get to heaven." They'll often reply, "Ask Jesus into your heart." I'll ask them, "Are you sure, because that is not in the Bible, and now I only have two and a half minutes to live." Thankfully, most people have a sense of humor, and they'll laugh as they stumble over every altar-call phrase they've ever heard. As time runs out, I'll ask, "What does someone need to believe to go to heaven?" "Um... they need to believe in Jesus?" "Believe what about Him? Mormons, Jehovah's Witnesses, Muslims, Catholics, and every other group that claims to respect Jesus has some type of belief in Him. What does a person need to believe? What is the gospel?" Often the answer comes in the form of a blank stare.

Again, in the inspired words of Paul, *"the gospel which I preached to you...that Christ died for our sins according to the Scriptures, and that He was buried, and that He was raised on the third day according to the Scriptures"* (1 Corinthians 15:1,3,4). When you evangelize, you must have a clear definition of the gospel. If you do not tell people that Jesus Christ died on the cross for our sins and rose from the dead, you have not presented the gospel. The gospel is not a promise that Jesus can make your life better, or that Jesus can come into your heart. Those phrases may mean something to a Christian who has been around church culture long enough, but they are not the gospel.

I once stood next to a pastor from a huge church as he shared the gospel with a teenager at a shopping mall. He told the teen, "You're a strong young man, you're intelligent; you should give your life to God. He could do a lot with a great guy like you." That was the pastor's "gospel message." There was no mention of sin, repentance, the cross, or the resurrection. It was just flattery and a challenge for the teen to give his life to God (with no explanation of why he should). I'm not even sure the young man knew that Jesus died on a cross; it never came up. The young man bowed his head and prayed a "sinner's prayer" and "asked Jesus into his heart." Sadly, there's a chance he still thinks he's a Christian today. If all the "gospel" he's ever heard was from that experience in the mall, he doesn't even know what the good news is.

Why It Matters

So what if Jesus died on a cross and rose from the dead two thousand years ago? How does that affect me? Sadly, many churchgoers I've spoken with cannot answer that. For the answer, we turn to the book of Romans:

> *"For all have sinned and fall short of the glory of God"*
> (Romans 3:23)

> *"But God demonstrates His own love toward us, in that while we were yet sinners, Christ died for us"* (Romans 5:8)

> *"For the wages of sin is death, but the free gift of God is eternal life in Christ Jesus our Lord"* (Romans 6:23)

Because of our sin, we deserve death, but God is merciful and He has provided a way for sinners to escape the punishment they deserve. When Jesus died on the cross, He took the punishment and paid the penalty of sin for all those who will believe. If you are a Christian, you broke God's moral law (the Ten Commandments), and Jesus paid your fine. This is what the cross is all about and why it matters tremendously to us today. In fact, there is nothing more important.

I spent a few years volunteering as a phone counselor for a youth crisis hotline. Teens would call with problems ranging from mild sadness to suicidal thoughts, and we would direct them to Christ and to resources for their particular situation (pregnancy counseling, drug rehabilitation, etc.). One memorable phone call was with a young man who had been very attentive to the gospel. He had a Christian background but had never trusted Christ. At the end of the conversation, I led him through a "sinner's prayer." He said all the right words and even promised to start going to church again. It was a great conversation—a victory! As our time came to a close, I asked, "So is there anything you have questions about or anything you want to say?" He said, "Yeah. I believe in everything you've said, except for the part about Jesus rising from the dead. I agree with the rest, though."

It was both surprising and sad. I was sad that the boy had rejected the resurrection, his only hope for salvation. I was also amazed that he had missed the point entirely. *"If Christ has not been raised, your faith is worthless; you are still in your sins"* (1 Corinthians 15:17). If Jesus is still in the grave, a dead Savior is no savior at all. If you are not trusting in the death and the resurrection of Christ, your sins have not been paid for and you are not a Christian. Romans 10:9 makes it clear what we need to believe for salvation: *"If you confess with your mouth Jesus as Lord, and believe in your heart that God raised Him from the dead, you will be saved."* That's why the resurrection matters.

When the cross and resurrection are excluded from a witnessing conversation, how is a sinner supposed to know what to believe to be granted eternal life? When a churchgoer makes the observation that Mormons, atheists, Muslims, and other non-Christian groups are "just as good" as Christians, and therefore will probably go to heaven, it reveals that they misunderstand the significance of the death and resurrection of Christ. All have sinned, and without Christ all are doomed to hell. The death and resurrection of Jesus Christ *must* be part of your gospel presentation.

Are People Really That Bad?

The concept of hell is offensive to a world that doesn't think about sin. Most of the people I speak with believe in heaven, and they also think most people are going there. They see no need for the death and resurrection of a Savior because they do not see themselves as sinners deserving of hell. From their perspective, maybe the members of ISIS and child molesters will go to hell, but that's about it. Most people aren't that bad.

The Bible presents a very different picture of mankind. I've often said to unbelievers, "If you don't think you deserve hell, then you don't understand how holy and righteous God is and how sinful and wicked you are." Yes, people are that bad. The prophet Isaiah described us long ago: *"For all of us have become like one who is unclean, and all our righteous deeds are like a filthy garment; and all of us wither like a leaf, and our iniquities, like the wind, take us away. There is no one who calls on Your name, who arouses himself to take hold of You; for You have hidden Your face from us and have delivered us into the power of our iniquities"* (Isaiah 64:6,7). In the New Testament, Paul adds, *"There is none who does good, there is not even one"* (Romans 3:12). These verses apply to everyone, including you and I. This is so important to communicate during a gospel presentation because if people don't see themselves as sinners, they will not see the value of the Savior.

Does sinning make someone a sinner, or does being a sinner make a person sin? Which came first, the sin or the sinner? According to the Bible, we are all born sinners, as King David recognized: *"Behold, I was brought forth in iniquity, and in sin my mother conceived me"* (Psalm 51:5). Humans are born with a sin nature and have a natural desire to sin. If you were to offer a hungry shark both a fish and a log, it would go for the fish. A shark can eat what it wants, but it chooses the fish because its actions are determined by its nature. Likewise, given the choice to sin or obey God, unbelievers will choose to sin because it's in their nature. Sharks don't eat every fish they see, and individuals do not participate in every sin, but humans by their sinful nature are drawn to sin.

Most men and women do not become axe murderers or arsonists, but being a sinner doesn't require extreme criminal behavior. Sin, according to the Bible, is failing to conform to God's perfect standard. As we noted earlier, *"For all have sinned and fall short of the glory of God"* (Romans 3:23).

Our Wicked Inheritance

The lost will often argue, "If we are born sinners, isn't our sin God's fault? Doesn't it stand to reason that God will not judge my sin since He made me this way?" This is a common question that you need to be ready to answer. It's an attempt to blame-shift our fault onto God. Our sin is not God's fault in any way.

Sin entered the human race when Adam and Eve disobeyed God in the garden of Eden (Genesis 3). God had given Adam very simple instructions: *"From any tree of the garden you may eat freely; but from the tree of the knowledge of good and evil you shall not eat, for in the day that you eat from it you will surely die"* (Genesis 2:16,17). That was the only restriction, but when pride is at work, even one restriction is way too many. Pride was Satan's downfall, and when he tempted Eve to disobey God, he went after her pride:

> *Now the serpent was more crafty than any beast of the field which the LORD God had made. And he said to the woman, "Indeed, has God said, 'You shall not eat from any tree of the garden'?" The woman said to the serpent, "From the fruit of the trees of the garden we may eat; but from the fruit of the tree which is in the middle of the garden, God has said, 'You shall not eat from it or touch it, or you will die.'" The serpent said to the woman, "You surely will not die! For God knows that in the day you eat from it your eyes will be opened, and you will be like God, knowing good and evil."* (Genesis 3:1–5)

Eve and Adam's next move had devastating results. We have felt the shockwave of their decision ever since. *"When the woman saw that the tree was good for food, and that it was a delight to the eyes, and that the tree was desirable to make one wise, she took from its fruit and ate; and she gave also to her husband with her, and he ate"* (Genesis 3:6). That verse contains the origin of sin in mankind. When they chose to disobey God, their sin brought death to mankind and a curse on all of creation.

So sin is not God's fault; it's man's. Adam, the first man, then passed his sinful nature on to his offspring, affecting the entire human race with his decision to sin. Paul explains, *"Therefore, just as through one man sin entered into the world, and death through sin, and so death spread to all men, because all sinned"* (Romans 5:12). According to the Bible, we are all born sinners. As we saw earlier, King David understood this, and we need to know it as well. We do not make ourselves sinners by sinning. As children of Adam, we have inherited his sin nature and have a propensity to sin. But we can't blame Adam either. As the verse above notes, "all sinned"—we have all personally committed sin.

Level Playing Field

Many of us have heard unbelievers say, "It's good that gang member [or convict or other really bad person] found Jesus; that's really good for them." Basically what they are saying is, "Those bad people need help, but since I'm not a bad person, I don't need help." This thinking is wrong. From a biblical perspective, everyone is bad since everyone has a sin nature. The same pride that blinded Adam and Eve continues to blind the self-righteous. Law-abiding citizens are only abiding by man's laws. No one keeps all of God's laws. Not your sweet grandma, not the pope, no one.

Some people may be nice sinners who do many good things, but all are sinners nonetheless. We are all on a level playing field when it comes to sin. The child molester and the man who runs the homeless shelter both deserve punishment for their sin. One person may sin in a way that is more heinous than someone else, but all have sinned, all fall short of God's glory (Romans 3:23).

Those who do not believe they are sinners are self-deceived, as God's Word makes clear: *"If we say that we have not sinned, we make Him a liar and His word is not in us"* (1 John 1:10). Everyone has sinned, and because of this, no one qualifies as a "good person" from God's point of view.

Let's say you ran an airline and you needed a pilot. You put the word out, and fifty candidates respond. One slight problem: all of them are blind. Which one do you hire? None (hopefully!), since none of the candidates qualify. Some candidates may know more about planes than others, some may be great people, but none of them qualify because blind pilots are not allowed to fly airplanes. Whether or not this seems fair has nothing to do with it. Airlines have requirements.

Not everyone wants to be a pilot, but most everyone wants to go to heaven when they die. God too has requirements. When John the apostle, under the inspiration of the Holy Spirit, spoke of the new heaven and earth he said, *"Nothing unclean, and no one who practices abomination and lying, shall ever come into it, but only those whose names are written in the Lamb's book of life"* (Revelation 21:27).

Sinners do not qualify for heaven. This applies to all sinners, not just "really bad" sinners. In my experience, it's often easier for me to approach a gang member or someone who is openly in sin for many reasons. Perhaps it's because I feel more compassion when the sin is evident. When I did ministry in Juvenile Hall, it was easy to tell the young men they are sinners, since they already knew it. Speaking to someone who was raised with good morals is much harder. Some people can tell you a million things wrong with everyone else, but they have a tough time admitting any sin of their own. As you evangelize, you must remember that the reason people need a Savior is not because they are unhappy, unsatisfied, or not living up to their full potential. Men and women need to be saved because they are sinners, and sinners are headed to hell.

Hell Awaits

After death, our existence continues. When the soul leaves the body, it is destined for either heaven or hell. These are the only two options in the afterlife as presented in the Bible. Jesus gave many warnings concerning hell, because He wanted us to understand just how horrible hell is. For example:

> *"If your hand causes you to stumble, cut it off; it is better for you to enter life crippled, than, having your two hands, to go into hell, into the unquenchable fire, where their worm does not die, and the fire is not quenched. If your foot causes you to stumble, cut it off; it is better for you to enter life lame, than, having your two feet, to be cast into hell, where their worm does not die, and the fire is not quenched. If your eye causes you to stumble, throw it out; it is better for you to enter the kingdom of God with one eye, than, having two eyes, to be cast into hell, where their worm does not die, and the fire is not quenched."*
>
> (Mark 9:43–48)

Many people choose to believe that hell is an analogy, or the fictitious location of a parable, or some other non-literal thing. Jesus does not share that view. He taught His disciples that hell was real. In the parable of the wheat and the tares, Jesus makes a clear distinction between the imagery of the parable and a real place called hell. In the parable, the tares are burned with fire. At the conclusion of the parable, Jesus explains what it all means: *"So just as the tares are gathered up and burned with fire, so shall it be at the end of the age. The Son of Man will send forth His angels, and they will gather out of His kingdom all stumbling blocks, and those who commit lawlessness, and will throw them into the furnace of fire; in that place there will be weeping and gnashing of teeth"* (Matthew 13:40–42). To clarify, just as the tares (parable) will be gathered by men (parable) and burned in fire (parable), the people (literal) will be gathered by angels (literal) and be burned with fire (literal).

Many other references to hell are found in the New Testament. *"For if God did not spare angels when they sinned, but cast them into hell and committed them to pits of darkness, reserved for judgment..."* (2 Peter 2:4). *"But for the cowardly and unbelieving and abominable and murderers and immoral persons and sorcerers and idolaters and all liars, their part will be in the lake that burns with fire and brimstone, which is the second death"* (Revelation 21:8).

Eternal Torment

In recent years, some so-called Christian Bible teachers have taught the false idea that hell is not eternal, but a place of temporal punishment. The Jehovah's Witnesses and other counterfeit Christian groups have been teaching this heresy for years, but now some churches teach this wickedness as well. It's an attractive idea to those who have a warped view of God. To those who imagine God as a nice grandpa in the sky, an eternity without consequence makes sense. Whatever the case, the Bible clearly presents hell as a place of conscious, eternal torment:

"And the smoke of their torment goes up forever and ever; they have no rest day and night"　　　　　(Revelation 14:11)

"And the devil who deceived them was thrown into the lake of fire and brimstone, where the beast and the false prophet are also; and they will be tormented day and night forever and ever"　　　　　(Revelation 20:10)

If a church claims that hell either does not exist or is not eternal, they did not learn that from the Bible. The Bible is clear on the issue. It's interesting that pastors who deny the existence of hell usually do not have a problem with a literal, eternal heaven. They find all kinds of ways to twist Scripture when it comes to hell, but heaven is never an issue. When describing the fate of the lost, Jesus said, *"These will go away into eternal punishment, but the righteous into eternal life"* (Matthew 25:46). We know hell is a real place for the same reason we know heaven is real—both were taught by Jesus. Hell is a horrible place. Some people cringe at the suggestion that they deserve to go there. This makes it difficult to bring it up, but we must warn people. As hard as it is, think of the alternative!

Years ago on a mission trip in Sudan, Africa, I was walking toward a field when a child grabbed my arm. He did not speak English, and he began pulling me in the opposite direction. I didn't know what he was doing and thought it was funny. I kept walking while he tugged at me and I figured I had made a new friend. Then a man approached me and said, "He is telling you not to go that way because that is a mine field." Can you imagine if that child had been too embarrassed to tell me about the danger? At that moment, I did not feel embarrassed or stupid (though I was both!). I was relieved and thankful for the warning.

Many times after I have explained sin, judgment, hell, and the gospel, people have responded by thanking me. Without Christ, people will perish. We should be willing to warn them. They may laugh at us or misunderstand us, but we must do what we can to pull them in the opposite direction. The truth about hell makes sense when presented in a caring way. We need to warn people regardless of our comfort level. The consequences are far too great.

God's Hell vs. God's Love

One of the main objections against hell is the false idea that God would never send anyone to such a horrible place forever, since God is love. This is just bad theology. Yes, God is love (1 John 4:8), but that's not all He is. He is also a God of judgment (Hebrews 9:27), wrath (Romans 1:18), righteousness (Psalm 11:7), and many other attributes. God's character is multifaceted. Humans are multidimensional as well. I have never met a person who is all love or all hate; people have many sides to their character. Focusing on any one of God's characteristics to the exclusion of others will lead to an idolatrous view of God.

Sadly, many churchgoers have bought into the lie that God is all about love, exclusively, all the time. In many churches, hell, sin, judgment, and other "negative" truths are seldom mentioned. This kind of teaching produces a warped, "love only" idea of God. Over the years while street preaching, I have been interrupted many times by "Christians" who are offended that I am telling people that God will send unrepentant sinners to hell. It's the strangest thing, because often they will admit that what I am saying is true, but they just don't think I should be telling people. They'll say, "You shouldn't focus on God's judgment; focus on His love because God is love." But without an understanding of the high cost of sin and the horror of hell, Jesus' death makes no sense to the lost and the cross is just a piece of jewelry. The love of Christ on the cross is best understood within the context of man's sinful state:

> *For while we were still helpless, at the right time Christ died for the ungodly. For one will hardly die for a righteous man; though perhaps for the good man someone would dare even to die. But God demonstrates His own love toward us, in that while we were yet sinners, Christ died for us.*
>
> (Romans 5:6–8)

God loves sinners so much that He sent Jesus to die on the cross to save them from the hell they deserve.

Repentance and Faith

Earlier we defined the gospel as the death and resurrection of Jesus Christ for our sins. The knowledge of sin and hell is important to understand as well. The next aspect of a biblical gospel presentation is the desired response. What does God want people to do when they hear the gospel? How did Jesus and the disciples call people to respond when they preached the gospel? They called people to repent and believe.

> *"Now after John had been taken into custody, Jesus came into Galilee, preaching the gospel of God, and saying, 'The time is fulfilled, and the kingdom of God is at hand; repent and believe in the gospel'"* (Mark 1:14,15)

Paul said—

"I did not shrink from declaring to you anything that was profitable, and teaching you publicly and from house to house, solemnly testifying to both Jews and Greeks of repentance toward God and faith in our Lord Jesus Christ"

(Acts 20:20,21)

Paul continually preached repentance—

"So, King Agrippa, I did not prove disobedient to the heavenly vision, but kept declaring both to those of Damascus first, and also at Jerusalem and then throughout all the region of Judea, and even to the Gentiles, that they should repent and turn to God, performing deeds appropriate to repentance"

(Acts 26:19,20)

People are saved when they respond to the gospel through repentance and faith (belief). In many verses you may notice that only one of the terms is used, either repentance or belief. When Paul preached on Mars Hill, he proclaimed that men must repent (Acts 17:30). Jesus told Nicodemus that whoever believes in Him has eternal life (John 3:16). So which is it, repentance or belief? Well, it's both. Like two sides of the same coin, repentance and faith are the same thing from different points of view. When we turn to Christ, we are turning away from ourselves, our opinion, our sin, and our control of our own life. This is repentance, a turning away from something. At the same time, we are turning toward someone: Christ. Paul described the church in Thessalonica as a group who had *"turned to God from idols to serve a living and true God"* (1 Thessalonians 1:9). They turned away from something and turned toward someone. This is the essence of belief; we go to the only one who can save us.

Faith Without Repentance?

When people hear the gospel without understanding sin, God's judgment, hell, and repentance, it can have devastating results. I have met many self-proclaimed Christians who live in open sin. One young man I spoke with had been living with his girlfriend for years in a sexual relationship. He knew sex outside of marriage was a sin. He was going to church regularly. He believed in hell. He knew all the right stuff, but he had this crazy idea that since he'd once prayed the "sinner's prayer," God had forgiven him once and for all and now he can sin all he wants. Sadly, many churches are producing "Christians" just like this lost young man.

If repentance is not mentioned in the context of the gospel and churchgoers are taught "all you need to do is believe," "just accept Jesus into your heart," or some other unbiblical nonsense, then you get so-called Christians living like unbelievers. Newsflash: many "Christians" live like unbelievers because they are unbelievers. Without repentance, you will not go to heaven. Jesus said, *"Unless you repent, you will all likewise perish"* (Luke 13:3). Many people who claim to be Christians are not being truthful, according to John: *"If we say that we have fellowship with Him and yet walk in the darkness, we lie and do not practice the truth"* (1 John 1:6).

Lordless Salvation?

Some churches mock what they call "Lordship salvation," where sinners are to submit to Christ as Lord as well as trust in Him as Savior (the biblical call to repentance and faith). Their alternative idea, "Lordless salvation," is this: you need to accept Jesus as your

Savior, and then at some point you can make Him your Lord. I would not be surprised if the fornicating young man I spoke with came from a church with this kind of teaching. In his mind, he had been saved by "accepting" Jesus as Savior, but as far as the Lord thing went...well, it got in the way of his promiscuity. It's interesting that he understood his sin and the need for a Savior, but if you're not going to follow Christ, why go to church? Why claim Him at all? Jesus warned, *"Not everyone who says to Me, 'Lord, Lord,' will enter the kingdom of heaven, but he who does the will of My Father who is in heaven will enter. Many will say to Me on that day, 'Lord, Lord, did we not prophesy in Your name, and in Your name cast out demons, and in Your name perform many miracles? And then I will declare to them, 'I never knew you; depart from me, you who practice lawlessness'"* (Matthew 7:21–23).

The idea that you can somehow separate Christ as Savior and Christ as Lord is foreign to the Bible. He is either both to you, or He is neither. If I was at your front door, and you were to tell me, "Eddie can come in, but Roman needs to stay out," I would need to stay out, because you can't have half of me. Jesus Christ is God; why do people think they can section Him off? If you reject Christ as your Lord, you reject Him, period. You can't have Jesus as Savior only, because if He is not your Lord, He is not your Savior.

I believe many pastors who teach this twisted version of the gospel will have hell to pay, literally. I also think they have some millstones waiting for them, as Jesus warned: *"Whoever causes one of these little ones who believe to stumble, it would be better for him if, with a heavy millstone hung around his neck, he had been cast into the sea"* (Mark 9:42).

One of the clearest warnings against the self-deception of "Christians" living a sinful lifestyle is found in 1 Corinthians 6. I have shown this passage to self-proclaimed "Christian" fornicators, homosexuals, drunks, and drug addicts: *"Or do you not know that the unrighteous will not inherit the kingdom of God? Do not be deceived; neither fornicators, nor idolaters, nor adulterers, nor effeminate, nor homosexuals, nor thieves, nor the covetous, nor drunkards, nor revilers, nor swindlers, will inherit the kingdom of God. Such were some of you; but you were washed, but you were sanctified, but you were justified in the name of the Lord Jesus Christ and in the Spirit of our God"* (1 Corinthians 6:9–11). Verse 11 shows the contrast between someone who is going to hell and someone who is not. Those who are saved are different—they have been washed and sanctified by God and are no longer engaged in a lifestyle of sin. Don't be self-deceived; if your life is marked by continual sin in any of the areas listed in 1 Corinthians 6:9,10, Jesus is not your Lord, and you are not His follower. Only obedient followers of Christ inherit the kingdom of God.

That doesn't mean Christians will always do everything Jesus says, 100 percent of the time, and never sin. No one can do that. But there's a big difference between a Christian who falls into sin and a self-deceived unbeliever who dives into sin. When Christians sin, they feel regret, they are convicted by the Holy Spirit, and they change as God sanctifies them over time. When unrepentant, self-deceived, counterfeit Christians sin, they make excuses and claim they are saved since they prayed a prayer or responded to an altar call. In my experience, these people are the hardest to explain the gospel to, because they think they already know the gospel. If only their pastor had preached repentance!

Perhaps they would not have followed Christ, but at least they would not be self-deceived. As you can see, what you say in a gospel presentation is critical. Sin, hell, the cross, the resurrection, repentance, and faith are all elements that must be explained. In the next chapter we will put it all together into a simple, practical format that will equip you to present the gospel to anyone, in any situation.

QUESTIONS FOR REFLECTION

1. Why is 1 Corinthians 15:1–4 such an important gospel verse?

2. Why can the "sinner's prayer" be a problem?

3. What do sinners need to be saved from?

4. Why is it important to include both the death and the resurrection of Christ in a gospel presentation?

5. What is the fate of those who do not repent and trust Christ during this life?

6. What are some verses stating that hell is eternal?

7. Can someone be saved without repentance? Explain your answer. _____

_____

_____

8. Is it possible to have Jesus as your Savior, but not your Lord? Why would anyone want to have this sort of arrangement with Christ? _____

_____

_____

_____

WATCH THIS! //

- Let's take a look at the results of bad gospel presentations and false conversions.
- Go to eddieroman.com and click Watch on the top menu.
- Watch the video labeled "Hypocrisy."

PRAYER POINT //

- Ask Christ to help you communicate the gospel clearly and biblically.

3

WHAT SHOULD I SAY?

John Piper sums up the gospel in one sentence: "The gospel is the news that Jesus Christ, the Righteous One, died for our sins and rose again, eternally triumphant over all his enemies, so that there is now no condemnation for those who believe, but only everlasting joy."[1] That is an excellent definition of the gospel! It's short, clear, and covers the main issues. So memorize that sentence, recite it to people, and they will get saved immediately, right? Boy, if only it worked that way. If you think evangelism is simply a matter of knowing what to say, I humbly suggest you run from that mindset as fast as possible. Yes, what you say is critical, but there's a whole lot more going on when the gospel is at work. There are at least three things that will hinder your efforts to reach the lost.

---

1   John Piper, "The Gospel in 6 Minutes," Desiring God, September 12, 2007 <desiringgod.org/articles/the-gospel-in-6-minutes>."

Hindrances to the Gospel

First of all, preaching the gospel to an unbeliever puts you right in the middle of a full-fledged war zone. You might be explaining the cross to a good friend, seated at an outdoor café on a sunny day with calming music playing in the background, but make no mistake—you are in a fierce battle. As we try to rescue souls out of Satan's kingdom, the Bible assures us our enemy is fighting us every step of the way: *"For our struggle is not against flesh and blood, but against the rulers, against the powers, against the world forces of this darkness, against the spiritual forces of wickedness in the heavenly places"* (Ephesians 6:12). We'll take a closer look at spiritual warfare in the context of evangelism in chapter 5.

Another thing to keep in mind as we share the gospel with our smiling friend at the café is the issue of the heart. Your friend might be all smiles on the outside, but the heart of the problem is the problem of the heart. According to God (who knows all hearts), *"The heart is more deceitful than all else and is desperately sick; who can understand it?"* (Jeremiah 17:9). As we covered in the previous chapter, people have a sin nature. That sin thing tends to get in the way when the gospel is presented. Jesus' parable of the sower and the soils in Mark chapter 4 shows that some people are just not going to receive the gospel for different reasons, all of which have to do with the heart. There is a battle going on within the heart of the unbeliever as you explain God's truth. You have a lot going against you, including...you.

In addition to the demonic hindrance of the gospel and the tendency of man to reject the things of God, you may be hindering your own evangelism. In this chapter, I will present a simple way to share the gospel, but before I do, you need to understand that evangelism must be done according to the Word of God. I'm not talking about using Bible verses when you speak (although that is important). I'm talking about the way you speak and the way you act with the lost. Your actions will determine much of what your words accomplish. *"Conduct yourselves with wisdom toward outsiders, making the most of the opportunity."* (Colossians 4:5).

Approach With Caution

I once lived up the street from a family of convicts—three generations of Mexican gang members, each of whom had done prison time. One day a car went speeding past their house while they were chillin' on the porch. The men jumped off the porch to yell at the driver to slow down. The car skidded to a halt. Bad move. The driver started arguing with the men. Worse move. The driver was then pulled out of his car and beaten severely. Welcome to the neighborhood.

My interaction with the family was different. We had something in common: a Rottweiler. I would walk my dog and politely say hi when I passed their house (they were always on the porch). They would pet my dog and fist-bump my little boy. They were always nice to us. They never beat me up in the street. There's a lot to be said about how you approach people.

You might not deal with gang members when you evangelize, but you will always deal with opposition. You must be wise. Holding a sign that says "God hates fags" is not wise (or biblical). Witnessing to your sleepy neighbor the morning after you blasted worship music all night with your window open is not wise. Your conduct speaks volumes before you even open your mouth. Ask yourself this simple question: is there anything about my behavior that is hindering my witness? An obvious example would be preaching the gospel while wearing an Ozzy Osbourne T-shirt. You may have the liberty in Christ to wear whatever T-shirt you want, but is it wise?

Your conduct matters, as does the way you speak. Paul went on to say, *"Let your speech always be with grace, as though seasoned with salt, so that you will know how you should respond to each person"* (Colossians 4:6). Some foods go down a lot easier with salt, and some truths go down much easier with grace. Many Christians are afraid to bring up the subjects of sin, judgment, hell, and Jesus because they are fearful that the conversation will turn into an argument. In my regular evangelism to strangers, I rarely face a person who gets upset when I bring up hard truths. I've spoken with homosexuals about their sin of homosexuality. I've informed hypocrites in the church that they need to repent and follow Christ. I've instructed thugs to leave their street gang and Mormons to depart from their false church. In spite of all the hard truth I've communicated, the amount of backlash I've received during these conversations is relatively small. Not to say people have never been mad at me, but for the most part, I do not get into heated arguments. I believe this is due to a section of Scripture the Lord impressed upon me early in my evangelism efforts:

The Lord's bond-servant must not be quarrelsome, but be kind to all, able to teach, patient when wronged, with gentleness correcting those who are in opposition, if perhaps God may grant them repentance leading to the knowledge of the truth,

and they may come to their senses and escape from the snare of
the devil, having been held captive by him to do his will.

(2 Timothy 2:24–26)

When you talk to people about Jesus, there is a chance they will oppose you. Before I became acquainted with this verse, I found myself getting dragged into arguments with unbelievers about all kinds of things. I usually had the perfect verse for the occasion, but the fact that I was arguing in an unkind way was blowing my witness. We must be kind, patient, and gentle. If you think you're exempt from all that because your personality is a certain way, you're wrong. Take a look at these qualities again. If they do not describe you, ask God to change you.

I went through about a year of God shaping my character in this area. It happened in Oceanside, California, during our weekly open-air preaching outreach. Many times while preaching, someone would mock or challenge me. I actually welcome the challenges; public debates are the perfect setting to answer common questions about God and proclaim the gospel to many who do not go to church. Public preaching, I've learned, is also a great way for a preacher to realize how impatient he is. When someone begins cussing at you and belittling Jesus Christ, the one who is everything to you, it can be tough. When you have explained the gospel to someone, and they are open and interested, showing signs of repentance, and their friend pulls them away because they have someplace they need to be, it's rough.

There are so many things that can happen during open-air preaching, and many of them are against you. Different personalities respond to opposition in various ways. I've seen street preachers mock the hecklers who oppose them. I've watched Christians destroy unbelievers with logic while maintaining an attitude of pride over those "dumb lost people." Some open-air preachers overpower their hecklers with a loud, angry voice. I was more of the "sarcastic comeback" type, turning opposing comments into a joke, making my opponent look stupid and moving on from there. All of these examples fall short of God's instruction to be kind and patient toward those with opposing views.

Thankfully, I have also witnessed great examples of open-air preaching. Scott Smith of School Master Ministries is a man who exemplifies the combination of truth and grace. Scott is regularly at secular universities, standing on a bench with a Bible in hand, proclaiming the gospel in the open air. As you can imagine, many students hate the Word of God, so Scott receives opposition on a regular basis. In the face of hatred and mocking, Scott answers opponents with Scripture, while keeping his composure and genuinely listening to the students. He exhibits care and concern for his audience, including the mockers. At the end of his preaching, he is often approached by students who have questions, and he gladly sits and talks for as long as necessary.

You may never open-air preach, but you can communicate truth in a kind way. If the Spirit of God lives within you, you are already equipped to act with kindness and patience: *"But the fruit of the Spirit is love, joy, peace, patience, kindness, goodness, faithfulness, gentleness, self-control"* (Galatians 5:22,23). Acting kindly toward others is a natural result of God's work in your life. There is no reason to change this during evangelism. We should be seeking to follow Christ in every area of life, including our outreach. Our evangelism is a result of obedience to Christ, so our conduct and speech during evangelism should be according to Christ. Jesus instructs us to "love your enemies and pray for those who persecute you" (Matthew 5:44). You will encounter enemies when you share the gospel with the lost. Make sure you love them.

Transitioning

How do you bring up the things of God? How do you go from, "How's college going?" to, "What do you think happens after you die?" My advice is to just bring it up. Fight the feelings of awkwardness, nervousness, and every other emotion that arises during those times and just say what you want to say. I think honesty is the best policy; being straightforward about what is on your mind is a good way to go. I prefer "kind directness," rather than trying to come up with one-liners that will get you into a spiritual conversation without the unbeliever even noticing. "This chicken tastes good...Hey, God created the chicken, and He's in heaven! Are you going to heaven or hell?" There's no need for that; just take the risk and bring it up.

Sometimes it will be awkward, and you'll feel the tension from the person you are talking to, but you will also be amazed how many people are very willing to talk about spiritual things. Many people are thinking about religious issues, but you will never know it unless you take a chance and bring it up. Witnessing to strangers and friends may seem insane, but the more you do it, the more you realize how many people are concerned about the afterlife. Don't be afraid to bring it up. They might not always agree with you, but many people are thinking about spiritual things.

Asking questions is a good way to take a conversation from the natural to the spiritual. It requires boldness, but remember,

"I can do all things through Him who strengthens me" (Philippians 4:13). Some good transition questions are: Do you ever think about God? Do you think there's a heaven? These questions can be asked of people you know well or not at all. They are non-judgmental questions; you are not accusing them of anything. Their answer will indicate whether they are open to conversation about spiritual things or not. If they answer, "Ummm, sometimes," that's good. If they jump up out of their seat and say, "You close-minded, anti-choice, bigoted jerk!," you are welcome to politely change the subject by saying, "Uh...how's work?"

All In or All Ashamed?

There's another beautiful aspect of being straightforward in bringing up the things of God—it communicates your love and dedication toward Him. It shows boldness in a culture that is overly concerned with political correctness. When you go against the grain and talk about Jesus Christ as the only way of salvation, it's an excellent way to honor God. We sing hymns such as "All to Jesus I surrender..." but do we live that way? Let people see that you are all for Jesus by bringing up the gospel. As Christians, we should never be ashamed of the gospel. If you are embarrassed to talk about Jesus, that may be the issue. *"For I am not ashamed of the gospel, for it is the power of God for salvation to everyone who believes, to the Jew first and also to the Greek. For in it the righteousness of God is revealed from faith to faith; as it is written, 'But the righteous man shall live by faith'"* (Romans 1:16,17). So often we need to share the gospel with someone who ought to be ashamed of their sin, yet we are the ones who are ashamed to bring up the gospel, the only thing that can help them. This should not be.

Look for opportunities to transition into spiritual conversations. After a weekend off work, ask your coworkers what they did over the weekend. Tell them you went to church, then ask if they go to church. When you're at the park watching your kids, strike up a conversation with another parent. Talk about how much your child likes Sunday school and ask them if they go to church anywhere. If you are looking for opportunities to talk about Jesus, you will find them.

Icebreakers

One of the easiest ways to get into a gospel conversation is by using a gospel tract. This can work with a friend or a stranger. Gospel tracts are small brochures that feature a short salvation message. Some are the size of a business card with a one-minute message; others are large and in-depth. They are perfect for breaking the ice because they do the transition work for you. Just hand a gospel tract to someone and ask, "Did you get one of these?" The person will usually ask, "What is it?" To which you can reply, "It's a gospel tract; it talks about God and stuff like that. Do you ever think about that stuff?" (I'm a simple man who uses simple words. Scholarly Bible words are not required when talking to non-seminary people.) Once they have the tract and have heard you mention God, you are now in a spiritual conversation. The transition work is done. They may choose to end the conversation, or they may share their deepest hopes and fears with you; you never know. Whatever the case, gospel tracts do the work of bringing up the most important subject in the world: salvation.

Law and Gospel

Over the years, churches and ministries have come up with different methods for presenting the gospel. Some of the more popular ones include Evangelism Explosion, Four Spiritual Laws, Two Ways To Live, and the Law and Gospel method (also known as The Way of the Master). I prefer the Law and Gospel approach. For an in-depth explanation of this method, see Ray Comfort's book *God Has a Wonderful Plan for Your Life*. I'll give you the short version.

Obviously, when hearing the gospel, people need to understand why they need the Savior. By using the Ten Commandments, you can easily show the lost their sin, and therefore their need for repentance, forgiveness, and salvation. Once the need is established, the work of Jesus Christ on their behalf becomes evident. It's a very simple concept many churches do not seem to understand. When "gospel preaching" is based on our desire for happiness, joy, fulfillment, or even worse, material things (as in the case with "health and wealth" preaching), it misses the point. Jesus did not come to make us happy. Happiness will usually occur as a result of understanding His work on the cross, but that's not the reason He died and rose from the dead. He died to pay for our sin. If that is not covered in your gospel presentation, you do a disservice to the lost person you are speaking with. Don't be afraid to address sin. It may be easier to talk about the happiness and fulfillment that will come as a result of salvation, but those things are not the issue. The issue is sin and it must be addressed.

How to Address Sin

Many unbelievers know the Bible verse, *"Do not judge"* (Matthew 7:1). It's only part of a verse, usually taken out of context and applied to anyone who confronts their sin. It's a good idea to memorize another verse on judging, *"Do not judge according to appearance, but judge with righteous judgment"* (John 7:24). The Bible does tell us to judge, but not according to appearance. If someone tells me it's wrong to judge, I usually agree that it would be a mistake for me to judge their heart by the way they look. I'll then tell them we can judge ourselves by looking at the Ten Commandments. Another common phrase is, "Only God can judge me." I always agree and add, "That's the problem, He is going to judge us." If I am speaking in a kind, respectful way, people usually agree. No one likes to be looked down upon. When you talk in a condescending manner, people notice. If you speak and listen as if you are chatting with a friend, you'll do fine. Just remember you are talking with a person who was created by the God you love. They are not the enemy; Satan is the enemy. They are not a prospective notch on your belt, a win for the ol' Facebook status or an evangelism conquest. They are a person headed for hell, in desperate need of salvation.

The Law and Gospel method is an excellent way to address sin. It allows unbelievers to realize they are sinners, deserving of hell. Also known as the Good Person Test, the Law and Gospel method consists of a series of simple questions. The Good Person Test is a track to run on for evangelism. You may be knocked off track with side issues, but you can always get right back on track and lead a person to Jesus Christ. As you go through the questions, observe how five of the Ten Commandments are used to help a person see their sin. I've included the answers I usually hear from unbelievers, to make this sample conversation understandable.

The Good Person Test, Part 1

Would you consider yourself to be a good person? The usual answer is: *(Yes.)*

Can I ask you some questions to see if you are a good person? *(Yes.)*

How many lies have you told in your life? *(A lot.)*

What do you call someone who tells lies? *(A liar.)*

Have you ever stolen something? *(Yes.)*

What do you call someone who steals things? *(A thief.)*

Have you ever used God's name in vain? *(Yes.)*

That's called blasphemy; it's very serious in light of who God is. Have you ever lusted after someone? *(Yes.)*

Jesus said, *"You have heard that it was said, 'You shall not commit adultery'; but I say to you that everyone who looks at a woman with lust for her has already committed adultery with her in his heart"* (Matthew 5:27,28). Have you ever been angry at someone? *(Yes.)*

Jesus said, *"You have heard that it was said to those of old, 'You shall not murder, and whoever murders will be in danger of the judgment.' But I say to you that whoever is angry with his brother without a cause shall be in danger of the judgment"* (Matthew 5:21,22, NKJV).

Now I can't judge you, but you've admitted that you're a liar, a thief, a blasphemer, an adulterer at heart, and a murderer at heart. Here's a serious question. If God judges you according to His Ten Commandments—that's what we've been looking at: you shall not lie, you shall not steal, etc.—will He find you innocent or guilty? *(Guilty.)*

If God finds you guilty, should He send you to heaven or hell? *(Hell.)*

Does that concern you? *(Yes.)*

We will continue the Good Person Test in a moment, but I'd like to comment on the first half of the test. So far we have focused on sin, and there is a good reason for this. Once someone has understood and admitted their sin, it then makes sense to them that a good God would send them to hell. Not because He's mean, not because His Word is too strict, but because guilty sinners deserve punishment. When a person sees their sin from God's perspective, they are ready for the gospel. Without the realization of their sin, people will not understand how or why the gospel matters. I saw an obvious example of this on the sidewalk in Old Town Temecula. A friend of mine walked up to a man and said, "Jesus loves you. He died for you." The man looked at my friend with a blank stare and said, "Okay." My friend tried to talk to him more, but the man said, "No, thanks; I'm good." In his mind, he is good, and that's the problem. That's what keeps many people away from Christ. People won't go to the doctor if they don't see themselves as sick, and people won't go to the Savior if they don't see themselves as sinners. When we take people through the Good Person Test, they are confronted with God's holiness and their sin. Once that is established, it's time to present the gospel.

The Good Person Test, Part 2

The last question asked up to this point was whether the person is concerned about being headed for hell. Sometimes people will say no, they are not concerned. This usually has more to do with pride than anything else. Some will claim they don't believe in God. We'll get into that in the next chapter, but for now, we'll continue our questioning with a person who admits to being concerned about going to hell.

If God finds you guilty, should He send you to heaven or hell? *(Hell.)*

Does that concern you? *(Yes.)*

Do you know what God did for you to save you from hell, even though you deserve to go there? *(Umm, Jesus died on the cross?)*

Yes. Do you understand why that matters, and how something that happened two thousand years ago applies to you? *(Not really.)*

I'm going to explain it, and then I want to get your thoughts, okay? *(Okay.)*

Imagine you are standing in a court of law, and you're guilty of a very serious crime. Eyewitnesses are present, your crime was captured on video, and you know you are in serious trouble. Just before they send you to prison, imagine the judge Himself gets up from His bench, takes off His robe and walks over to you. He says, "You deserve punishment, but I care about you so much, I'm going to pay your fine." Since your crime is being paid for, you are free to go; the law no longer has a hold on you. When Jesus died on the cross, He was paying for the sin of all those who would believe on Him. You broke the law, and Jesus paid your fine. Does that make sense? *(Yes.)*

The Bible says, *"For God so loved the world, that He gave His only begotten Son, that whoever believes in Him shall not perish, but have eternal life"* (John 3:16). *"For the wages of sin is death, but the free gift of God is eternal life in Christ Jesus our Lord"* (Romans 6:23). The way you receive what Jesus did on the cross is through belief. Turn from your sin and trust in Jesus. The Bible uses a word for this: "repentance." It means to turn, and it begins in the mind. Right now you have something in your mind, an idea about God, the afterlife, and how you might get to heaven. Maybe you are trusting in your good works or the Virgin Mary or some other religious thing. To repent means to turn from that belief and trust in Jesus Christ, the fact that He died on the cross for your sins and rose from the dead. If you do that, God will forgive your sins and give you the gift of everlasting life. See, our problem on Judgment Day will be that we're sinners who lack the righteousness required to enter heaven. When we put our faith in Christ, His righteousness is placed on us, and God sees us as perfect. We can never be perfect on our own, but when we trust Christ, God sees us as perfect. Turn from your sin, and put your faith in Jesus Christ alone for your salvation.

Mission Accomplished

At this point, the gospel presentation is over, since the gospel has been presented. Some Christians may wonder if they need to "seal the deal" or "go for the closer." Often this is done by leading someone in a "sinner's prayer," or asking if the person wants to "accept Jesus." While I wouldn't say it is always wrong to do that, I would point out that it is not biblical. That is, you do not find either a "sinner's prayer" or an invitation to "receive Jesus" anywhere in the Bible. When the Bible presents the gospel presentations of Jesus and the disciples, it usually ends simply with the command to repent and believe. Unbelievers are never invited to recite a prayer or ask Jesus into their heart. The verse that is often used to support "asking into the heart" is Revelation

3:20: *"Behold, I stand at the door and knock; if anyone hears My voice and opens the door, I will come in to him and will dine with him, and he with Me."* Based on this verse, preachers have said, "Jesus stands at the door of your heart, and you need to ask Him to come in." The problem with that interpretation is the context. In Revelation 3, Jesus is talking to His church, not to unbelievers. He is telling Christians to repent of being lukewarm. Since Jesus is not speaking to unbelievers within the context of a gospel presentation, we shouldn't use it that way.

So how should you end a gospel presentation? I believe you should call people to come to Christ within the context of the setting you are in and the person's situation. If I'm talking with a Mormon, I might say, "I know it would be hard to leave the Mormon church and follow the real Jesus Christ, but that's what you need to do. That's what repentance would look like in your situation. Trust in Christ alone for salvation, not the false teachings of the Mormon church." I once had a young unmarried couple listen to a very long gospel presentation. I explained the gospel from many different angles until I was sure they understood. I ended by telling them that they need to figure out what's more important, having sex with each other or following Christ and gaining eternal life. I added that if they pray to ask God for forgiveness but continue living in fornication, they are just deceiving themselves and their prayer will not do them any good. I spoke in a nice tone of voice, but I told them the truth. Had I told them to "ask Jesus into their heart," they may have continued in their self-deception. People must repent, or they will perish, according to Jesus (Luke 13:3). If you must use a popular phrase like "receive Christ," just make sure they understand what repentance is.

At the end of Paul's epic gospel presentation on Mars Hill, he concluded his message with a call to repentance. Paul said, *"Therefore having overlooked the times of ignorance, God is now declaring to men that all people everywhere should repent, because He has fixed a day in which He will judge the world in righteousness through a Man whom He has appointed, having furnished proof to all men by raising Him from the dead"* (Acts 17:30,31). In this instance, Paul simply presented the truth and the required response, then his listeners thought about what he said and reacted on their own. *"Now when they heard of the resurrection of the dead, some began to sneer, but others said, 'We shall hear you again concerning this.' So Paul went out of their midst. But some men joined him and believed, among whom also were Dionysius the Areopagite and a woman named Damaris and others with them"* (Acts 17:32–34). Paul did not call people to come forward for an invitation time, but the response came later as *"some men joined him and believed"* (Acts 17:34). He preached the gospel and let the chips fall as they may. So, while it's not wrong to ask for a response right then, neither is it required. Your goal should be to explain the gospel. If they understand the gospel, you've done your job.

Delayed Fruit

It would be great to see the results of our evangelism efforts, but this doesn't always happen. In fact, many believers are faithful to evangelize for years before they see any fruit. The prophet Jeremiah preached for *forty years* without seeing any fruit from his labors! His faithfulness to God's calling is a tremendous example. Are you willing to do what is right, regardless of the results? Faithful evangelists labor out of love and obedience to

God, not out of a desire to see results. The Holy Spirit works out His agenda on His timeline, not ours.

Years ago I dropped my car off at a repair shop and the mechanic gave me ride home. The drive was about ten minutes, so I took the opportunity to ask him if he went to church anywhere. He said no, and didn't seem interested. I began talking about my church and then transitioned into the Good Person Test. He was quiet, but went along with it, nodding his head as he drove, watching the road in silence. It was awkward, but at the end of the trip he had heard the gospel. I thanked him for the ride and life went on.

A couple years later I was back at the garage with another car problem. The same mechanic approached me with excitement and began telling me how he had become a Christian, and how it all started with our drive home. He said he had already been thinking about his drinking problem that day as well as other negative aspects of his life. God used that drive home to capture his attention. Soon after, he found a church in his neighborhood and began reading the Bible. He also shared that he was now serving in the youth ministry at his church. It was a huge blessing and encouragement for me, as well as a reminder that God is in control of salvation; we are simply His workers in the field.

In the parable of the seed, Jesus says something that everyone involved in evangelism needs to remember: *"The kingdom of God is like a man who casts seed upon the soil; and he goes to bed at night and gets up by day, and the seed sprouts and grows—how, he himself does not know"* (Mark 4:26,27). If you can remember the simple concept that God saves people on His timeline, it can take some of the pressure off your evangelism efforts. How foolish it would be for a farmer to plant a seed and then become frustrated because it doesn't sprout immediately. If your uncle doesn't repent after you explain the gospel over Thanksgiving dinner, keep praying for him, and remember, God is in control.

Condition of the Soil

Just prior to the parable of the seed, Jesus explains a related parable. The parable of the sower and the soils is another great truth to keep in mind concerning evangelism. The main thing to grasp is that people respond to the gospel in various ways for different reasons. Keep that in mind as you read this parable as told by Jesus in Matthew chapter 13:

> *"Behold, the sower went out to sow; and as he sowed, some seeds fell beside the road, and the birds came and ate them up. Others fell on the rocky places, where they did not have much soil; and immediately they sprang up, because they had no depth of soil. But when the sun had risen, they were scorched; and because they had no root, they withered away. Others fell among the thorns, and the thorns came up and choked them out. And others fell on the good soil and yielded a crop, some a hundredfold, some sixty, and some thirty. He who has ears, let him hear."* (Matthew 13:3–9)

> *"Hear then the parable of the sower. When anyone hears the word of the kingdom and does not understand it, the evil one comes and snatches away what has been sown in his heart. This is the one on whom seed was sown beside the road. The one on whom seed was sown on the rocky places, this is the man who hears the word and immediately receives it with joy; yet he*

has no firm root in himself, but is only temporary, and when affliction or persecution arises because of the word, immediately he falls away. And the one on whom seed was sown among the thorns, this is the man who hears the word, and the worry of the world and the deceitfulness of wealth choke the word, and it becomes unfruitful. And the one on whom seed was sown on the good soil, this is the man who hears the word and understands it; who indeed bears fruit and brings forth, some a hundredfold, some sixty, and some thirty." (Matthew 13:18–23)

Sowers of Seed

Our hope is in the power of the seed, which is *"the living and enduring word of God"* (1 Peter 1:23), not in our planting skills. Yes, we should hone our skills, but ultimately God causes the growth. We are to preach the Word and leave the results to God. When we view evangelism in this manner, it's easier to think long term and be patient with the process. Your sister may have rejected the gospel years ago, but there's still hope. Just keep praying and working the field. You have no idea what God is doing in her life; she may be nearing harvest time. We should never write people off. Be content, knowing that Jesus is Lord over salvation.

When we try to rush a decision for Christ, we overlook another important aspect of sowing seed. Not all of the soils are properly prepared. Jesus explained that those who are the rocky soil *"hear the word, immediately receive it with joy; and they have no firm root in themselves, but are only temporary; then, when affliction or persecution arises because of the word, immediately they fall away"* (Mark 4:16,17). I have seen people immediately respond to an evangelism message, only to reject Christianity later. What happened? According to Jesus, the word never actually took root. They might have looked like a saved person, but as time passed the truth was revealed—they were not truly saved: *"They went out from us, but they were not really of us; for if they had been of us, they would have remained with us; but they went out, so that it would be shown that they all are not of us"* (1 John 2:19).

Farmers Can Be Boring

Another thing I love about these parables is the aspect of the seed sower or the farmer. When you picture a farmer, you usually do not think of a dynamic speaker or an outgoing personality. You probably think of a humble, hardworking man on a tractor, just doing his job. It might be a tedious job, but it's an important job carried out by down-to-earth people. We are not gospel salesmen; we are farmers. Many people think that evangelism requires an outgoing, talkative personality. That is not true. An energetic personality may help in the area of preaching, but most evangelism is not preaching. If you can talk to a Christian friend, you can talk to an unbeliever.

Communication skill does not determine truth. A slow, monotone speaking person can present the same truth that a hyper radio host can. Communicating the gospel is simply explaining that Jesus died for our sins and rose again. It's neither a show nor a performance and showmanship is not required. If you have an outgoing personality, that is a blessing you can use to reach people. If you consider yourself a boring person, that is not a problem; God is not limited by your personality. In some cases, people may prefer listening to a soft-spoken, shy person rather than a talkative, polished speaker. God will use you just as you are. Just be faithful to sow that seed.

QUESTIONS FOR REFLECTION

1. Read Colossians 4:5,6. Is there anything about your behavior that could be hindering your witness for Christ? If so, what would it take to change your behavior? _____

   _____

   _____

   _____

2. According to 2 Timothy 2:24–26, what should our attitude be toward unbelievers? _____

   _____

   _____

3. In Romans 1:16, Paul says he is not ashamed of the gospel. Do you sometimes feel that unbelievers look down on you because you are a Christian? Does this bother you? Are you ashamed of the gospel? If so, how can you overcome that?

   _____

   _____

   _____

   _____

4. Why must we address sin when we explain the gospel? _____

   _____

   _____

5. Why is it important to use the law before presenting the gospel? _____

   _____

   _____

6. In the salvation of souls, what part is our responsibility and what part is God's? _____

_____

_____

7. If you explain the gospel to someone and they do not respond, have you failed? Why or why not? _____

_____

_____

8. Why is it important to see yourself as a sower of seed, rather than a gospel salesman? _____

_____

_____

WATCH THIS!

- Go to eddieroman.com and click Watch on the top menu.
- Watch the video labeled "Are You a Good Person?"
- This is a simple way to present the gospel.

PRAYER POINT

- Pray that God would help you conduct yourself in the best way possible toward unbelievers.

4

GIVING A DEFENSE

Without Christ, people are dead in sin. Before Jesus saved you, *"you were dead in your trespasses and sins, in which you formerly walked according to the course of this world, according to the prince of the power of the air, of the spirit that is now working in the sons of disobedience. Among them we too all formerly lived in the lusts of our flesh, indulging the desires of the flesh and of the mind, and were by nature children of wrath, even as the rest"* (Ephesians 2:1–3). What an insightful description of the lost! Unregenerate people are not just ignorant of the things of God; they are actively living against Him, following their nature. In the opening chapter of Colossians, the lost are described as *"alienated and hostile in mind, engaged in evil deeds"* (Colossians 1:21). No wonder evangelism can be such a battle!

In any fight, you need to have a good defense. Apologetics is the branch of Christian study that deals with defending the faith.

It comes from the Greek word *apologia*, which means "speech in defense." A verse that encourages us in apologetics is found in 1 Peter 3:15, where we're told to *"sanctify Christ as Lord in your hearts, always being ready to make a defense to everyone who asks you to give an account for the hope that is in you, yet with gentleness and reverence."* It's important to be ready and able to defend the gospel message against attacks. Whether it's a Catholic who asserts that you must do good works to earn your way to heaven or an atheist who ridicules you for following the "imaginary man in the sky," you need to be ready to make a defense.

No Excuses

As we looked at in chapter 1, many people are afraid to talk to non-Christians about the gospel out of fear. A main reason for this is pride: we don't want to look stupid. After Rave Girl shut me down, I felt stupid, and I didn't want to go through that again. Looking back, I realize I could have just smiled and continued handing out gospel tracts to other people. Following Christ should include a mind set on following Him regardless of the opposition. Shamefully, I let my pride and fear of man (and woman) get the best of me.

Another way pride manifests itself is when people refuse to evangelize because they don't know enough. They fear looking foolish or ignorant when they encounter questions they can't answer. Recently some Jehovah's Witnesses came to our door, and I was trying to show them where Jesus spoke about hell. I had one of them to turn in his Bible to Matthew 24. When we couldn't find the Scripture I was after, I realized it was in chapter 25.

I looked at him and smiled and said, "I meant 25." I looked stupid and felt stupid (and was stupid) for a moment, but we moved on. That's what happens when imperfect people do battle. In humility, realize you will make mistakes, you will mess up, and you will not know everything. Thankfully, you don't need to know it all. I once watched a new believer read a small gospel tract out loud in public. A group of young men and women stopped and listened, and they ended up getting into a great conversation about God. It was unbelievable!

Remember the woman at the well in John chapter 4? I'll give you the quick version: Samaritan lady with waterpot wonders why a Jewish man is talking to her. The Jewish man turns out to be Jesus. The lady says some things that indicate she knows a little about God, but not much. Jesus tells her He's the expected Messiah. The woman, still not knowing a whole lot, *"left her waterpot, and went into the city and said to the men, 'Come, see a man who told me all the things that I have done; this is not the Christ, is it?'"* (John 4:28,29). And the men responded: *"They went out of the city, and were coming to Him"* (John 4:30).

The woman at the well did not know much, but she knew enough to lead people to Christ. If you are a Christian, you know what the gospel is, and that is enough to lead people to Jesus. God has not commanded us to know everything, but He has commanded His followers to *"go into all the world and preach the gospel to all creation"* (Mark 16:15). Scripture memory and apologetics will help significantly, and each of us should learn all we can, but never use your lack of knowledge as an excuse to opt out of evangelism.

//

never use your lack of knowledge as
an excuse to opt out of evangelism

\\

The Best Motivation to Learn

Evangelism is a great motivator for Scripture memory and apologetics. There is nothing quite like being asked a difficult question when you don't know the answer—it's a great incentive to study the Bible and Christian books that address that particular issue. When I'm asked a question I can't answer, I make it my goal to find the answer. There was a time when I didn't know how to respond to criticisms of God, such as, "Your God is evil; He drowned all those innocent people in Noah's flood," or, "How can Jesus be God if He prays to God?" I can answer those now, mainly because I need to, as the same questions tend to resurface again and again.

Thankfully, skills are something each one of us can acquire. I don't happen to be skilled at ocean rescue. I go to the beach, I've sailed in boats, but I don't know what the Coast Guard knows because that's not my job. Although I once saved a kid who was going down with his BMX bike after jumping it into a lake (long story), I am not a water rescue professional. However, if I were out on the ocean each day, scanning the surface for signs of trouble, I would want to know everything I could about rescuing people. As we saw in 1 Peter 3:15, apologetics is part of the Christian's job description—we are to always be ready. The seas we navigate are the stormy waters of unbelief, false religion, idolatry, and demonic influence. We must become skilled at Scripture so we can *"contend earnestly for the faith which was once for all delivered to the saints"* (Jude 1:3). The better we become at apologetics, the more useful we will be in the hands of our Lord. Souls are at stake, and Christ will use His people to reach the lost. Let's do everything within our power to make ourselves useful as we reach out to the people around us. They are drowning in sin, and their only hope is Jesus Christ. In this chapter, I will present some information that can help you, but the real learning will begin when you become actively engaged in evangelism.

Believe the Bible

One of the simplest things you can do in the area of apologetics is this: believe the Bible. What do I mean by that? You're a Christian; you already believe the Bible, right? Well, I would hope so, but when contending for the faith, it is common for Christians to get caught up in useless arguments over things that come down to belief. Take Noah's Ark for example. It's a crazy story, the thought that a small family along with two of each kind of animal walked onto a boat and sailed to safety, while all the rest of the world drowned. How did all those animals fit on the ark? Christians often try to explain how it could have happened with baby animals and hibernation. My question is this: why are we giving unbelievers a reason to view Bible stories as natural and non-miraculous?

why are we giving unbelievers a
reason to view Bible stories as natural
and non-miraculous?

When we try to explain miraculous Bible stories with natural means, we forget two important things. First, they are miraculous. Noah's Ark and Jonah's fish encounter were both made possible by an all-powerful God who does miracles. No natural explanation is necessary. Second, when we attempt to help an unsaved, non-spiritual person understand the things of God, it is often futile. Unbelievers do not have the capability to understand spiritual truths, as Paul points out: *"A natural man does not accept the things of the Spirit of God, for they are foolishness to him; and he cannot understand them, because they are spiritually appraised"* (1 Corinthians 2:14). Do you believe that part of the Bible? Trying to explain spiritual truths to an unbeliever is like trying to explain the color blue to a man who was born blind. In both cases, they simply do not have the capacity to understand. How would you explain blue to a blind man? Would you tell him it looks like the feeling of cold? That might mean something to you since you have seen blue and understand why it's associated with cold temperatures. But how would someone who is blind make that association? He wouldn't, because he couldn't.

When entering into gospel conversations with non-Christian friends, family, and strangers, you will get hit with all sorts of arguments. Remember to believe the Bible's description of the lost. People are not lost because evolution seems scientific, or because they were brought up in a country where an Eastern religion is prevalent, or because their parents were hypocrites. Sure, those things can confuse people and distract them from the truth, along with many other issues that fight against the gospel, but they are not the main reasons people are lost. The main reason is always spiritual, never physical or intellectual. Lost people are dead spiritually, under the influence of Satan and bound to their sin nature. God described it clearly through the apostle Paul when he addressed the Ephesian church in Ephesians 2:1–3 (which we read earlier).

That's why we need to make sure the goal of our apologetics is to clear a path for the gospel. Defending the faith and answering questions biblically is a great thing, but never stop there. Use apologetics as a way to share the gospel and bring people to Christ. God understands the nature of mankind far better than we do. He has described why people reject the things of God, and thankfully, He has also shown us the answer to their problem, as Paul goes on to explain:

> *But God, being rich in mercy, because of His great love with which He loved us, even when we were dead in our transgressions, made us alive together with Christ* (by grace you have been saved), *and raised us up with Him, and seated us with Him in the heavenly places in Christ Jesus, so that in the ages to come He might show the surpassing riches of His grace in kindness toward us in Christ Jesus. For by grace you have been saved through faith; and that not of yourselves, it is the gift of God; not as a result of works, so that no one may boast.* (Ephesians 2:4–9)

Be Skeptical of Skeptics

During a gospel conversation, an atheist may say, "Don't use the Bible, I don't believe in it." That's understandable; if I were an enemy of God, I wouldn't want people using His Word on me either! Never allow a skeptic to hinder you from using the Bible when you talk about God. The Word is your sword, so never give it up during battle. I keep quoting from the Bible as I'm talking to them.

When people claim they do not believe in God, I usually keep talking about God as long as they will allow me to. If our discussion is civil and they are not closed-minded, the conversation can continue. Why do I do this? I speak as if God exists and the Bible is true—because God exists and the Bible is true. Remember what I said about believing the Bible when you do apologetics? That applies here. I don't get into arguments about the existence of God and I don't try to convince people that God exists because according to the Bible, they know He exists. They may be deceived, they might be in denial, but deep down they know. According to the Bible, they are suppressing the knowledge of Him.

For the wrath of God is revealed from heaven against all ungodliness and unrighteousness of men who suppress the truth in unrighteousness, because that which is known about God is evident within them; for God made it evident to them. For since the creation of the world His invisible attributes, His eternal power and divine nature, have been clearly seen, being understood through what has been made, so that they are without excuse. For even though they knew God, they did not honor Him as God or give thanks, but they became futile in their speculations, and their foolish heart was darkened. Professing to be wise, they became fools, and exchanged the glory of the incorruptible God for an image in the form of corruptible man and of birds and four-footed animals and crawling creatures.

Therefore God gave them over in the lusts of their hearts to impurity, so that their bodies would be dishonored among them. For they exchanged the truth of God for a lie and worshiped and served the creature rather than the Creator, who is blessed forever. Amen. (Romans 1:18–25)

Before you put a lot of time into "proving" the existence of God, understand that people suppress the truth. God has made His existence evident to all, and because of this, people are without excuse.

Sye Ten Bruggencate is a skilled presuppositional apologist with excellent questions for atheists. He often asks them, "If I could prove to your satisfaction that God exists, would you worship Him?" What a great question! I have asked that same question of atheists many times, and guess what the usual answer is? No. I've also asked atheists, "If I can show you the Bible is true and God is real, will you repent of your sin, pray to Him, and come to church with me on Sunday?" The answer is usually no. Ray Comfort says, "Atheists can't find God for the same reason thieves can't find a police officer. They aren't looking." Truth suppression is what sinful people do when they're hiding from God. Again, our battle is not primarily intellectual; it is spiritual.

If an atheist (or anyone else) communicates that they do not want to talk about God, I usually grant them that request. If someone is mocking God or apparently angry with Him, I'll usually get out of the conversation. While I do care about rabid God-haters, I also try to follow Jesus' advice: *"Do not give what is holy to dogs, and do not throw your pearls before swine, or they will trample them under their feet, and turn and tear you to pieces"* (Matthew 7:6). If you have a friend or relative who is hostile toward the things of God, pray for the person, knowing that Jesus died for us when we were His enemies: *"For if while we were enemies we were reconciled to God through the death of His Son, much more, having been reconciled, we shall be saved by His life"* (Romans 5:10). God saves haters.

American Idols

Atheists make up a tiny percentage of the unbelievers in the world. Most people have some belief in something they call "god." Those who claim to believe in "a god," but not the God of the Bible, are practicing a form of idolatry. This includes many individuals who attended Christian churches for years but were never born again. A "Christian" who does not believe that God would create hell does not believe in the God of the Bible. A churchgoer who believes that all religions will lead people to heaven is not following God but rather a false god that they have created in their mind. The Scriptures clearly teach that the one true God sends people to hell. According to God, the only way to heaven is through repentance and faith in Jesus Christ. Does God forgive idolatry? He sure does (1 Corinthians 6:9–11). I'm glad, since I once practiced religion as an idolater.

I've met unbelievers who know the Bible very well, but knowledge of the truth does not guarantee salvation. In addition to many who have heard the truth and rejected it, those in false religions have been taught a twisted version of the truth. Mormons, Jehovah's Witnesses (JWs), Muslims, Buddhists, and most other religious groups have an incorrect version of God, Jesus, and salvation. There are many great apologetics authors and ministries with in-depth material on each of these groups.

I think it's great to know what the false religions teach, but it's more important to know what the Bible teaches. Before you spend tons of time learning about every different group's beliefs, get a good grasp on the Bible; it will be way more helpful. For example, every false religion attacks the Trinity. For this reason, I'd like to spend a little time on this mind-blowing attribute of our God.

An Incomprehensible God

There is something we should remember when approaching big doctrines like the Trinity—God is incomprehensible. We cannot fully understand everything about Him. We can know what He has revealed about Himself to us in His Word, but beyond that, we don't know much about Him. Scripture tells us that *"the secret things belong to the LORD our God, but the things revealed belong to us and to our sons forever"* (Deuteronomy 29:29). Zophar put it this way when challenging Job, *"Can you discover the depths of God? Can you discover the limits of the Almighty? They are high as the heavens, what can you do? Deeper than Sheol, what can you know? Its measure is longer than the earth and broader than the sea"* (Job 11:7–9). The answer, of course, is no, we can't know any of that stuff. Don't ever be ashamed to admit that. Many false teachers started off as Bible students who didn't understand a truth and couldn't handle it. Hell is a hard truth that Bible teacher Charles Russell couldn't understand and wouldn't accept. Instead of humbly admitting God knows more than he does, he disregarded the truth about hell and started the Jehovah's Witnesses. Sadly if he did not repent he is now facing the hell he disregarded.

I once was witnessing to a Muslim lawyer and his wife near Disneyland. He started drilling me with questions about the Trinity. "How could God die? If Jesus was God, why did He not know some things?" He claimed that he couldn't understand why we believe this and asserted that God would not do things that we cannot understand. I questioned his assertion and asked him why he thinks men should be able to comprehend God. Why in the world would finite humans totally understand an infinite God and why He does everything He does? He stopped to think about this. I explained that God is incomprehensible; it makes sense that we can't make sense of everything He does. The man smiled and agreed. He confided in me that he was not a very good Muslim. I took him through the Good Person Test, and he heard the gospel for the very first time. He thanked me for taking the time to explain it all, we shook hands, and they left to catch a movie. God is incomprehensible, and it's good to acknowledge it.

The Dreaded Doctrine of the Trinity

Some believers cry, "Noooooo! Don't make me try to understand the Trinity!" Are you one of those who has accepted the "fact" that you will never understand the Trinity, so you shouldn't even try? I would agree this doctrine is not simple, but there is much we can know about the Trinity. God has not revealed everything about Himself, but He sure has shown us a lot! Unfortunately, there is a myth within Christian churches that says, "The doctrine of the Trinity is just too hard to understand, so don't worry about it." I wonder who invented that myth—lazy preachers or the

Mormons? In any case, it's just not true. It might take longer than a day for you to get a good grasp of it, but you can do it. Some truths are more complex than others, but God has given you a mind, and you are to love Him with it: *"You shall love the LORD your God with all your heart, and with all your soul, and with all your mind"* (Matthew 22:37). One way to love God with your mind is by learning about Him.

If you talk with a lot of unbelievers, you will hear all kinds of supposed reasons you believe in the Trinity. According to them, it's a result of your upbringing, or a church council decision from long ago, or some other unprovable issue. It's important to remember that the reason Christians believe in the Trinity is that it's clearly taught in the Bible. If you believe the Bible, you will believe the Trinity, period. If people claim to believe in the Bible, but follow an anti-biblical system (Jehovah's Witnesses, Mormons, Oneness Pentecostals, etc.), they will have a difficult time untangling the lies they have learned concerning the Trinity. In the Bible you will find the following truths:

- There is one God.
- God speaks of Himself in the plural sense.
- The Father is God.
- Jesus is God.
- The Holy Spirit is God.
- The Father, the Son, and the Holy Spirit have existed together throughout eternity.
- The Father, Son, and Holy Spirit are divine and equal in nature.
- The Father, Son, and Holy Spirit have different roles.

James White, in his book *The Forgotten Trinity*, gives an excellent definition of the Trinity: "Within the one Being that is God, there exists eternally three coequal and coeternal persons, namely, the Father, the Son, and the Holy Spirit."[2]

This definition is worth memorizing. It's short, and it covers the main issues. First of all, it addresses the main reason people are confused about the Trinity: the difference between a being and a person. Once you understand this aspect of the Trinity, you will be able to deal with most of the criticism directed toward this great truth of the Bible.

Being vs. Person

James White has been debating false teachers since 1990. In formal debates with Mormons, Muslims, Jehovah's Witnesses, Oneness Pentecostals, and many other errant groups, James has heard all kinds of arguments against the Trinity. According to James, the issue usually has more to do with misunderstandings than anything else. He says, "The single greatest reason people struggle with the doctrine of the Trinity is miscommunication. It is very rare that anyone argues or debates about the true doctrine of the Trinity. Most arguments that take place at the door, or over coffee, or at the workplace involve two or more people fighting vigorously over two or more misrepresentations of the doctrine itself. It is no wonder, so many encounters create far more heat than they do light."[3]

One misrepresentation is the claim that the doctrine is self-contradictory or illogical. "How can God be one and three at the same time? That's a contradiction. Therefore it cannot be true."

---

2   James R. White, *The Forgotten Trinity* (Minneapolis: Bethany House Publishers, 1998), 26.

3   Ibid., 23.

Some well-meaning Christians have answered this by saying, "God is beyond logic." That's not a great answer since logic is a reflection of the way God thinks. He might be incomprehensible, but that is different from being illogical. If the Bible taught that "one being" exists as "three beings," or "one person" is "three persons," that would be illogical, but that's not what it says. One being (God) exists as three persons (Father, Son, and Holy Spirit).

It's important to make the distinction between a being and a person. An inanimate rock is not a living being, nor is it a person. A tree is a living being, but a tree has no person within its being. Within a human being there exists one person, and within the being of God there exists three persons. God is different from us.

One God

One of the most fundamental truths about the God of the Bible is that He alone is God and He is one. In Deuteronomy 6:4 Moses proclaims, *"Hear, O Israel! The LORD is our God, the LORD is one!"* Christians are monotheists—we believe in one God. Throughout the Bible, God makes it a point to remind us of this: *"Thus says the LORD, the King of Israel and his Redeemer, the LORD of hosts: 'I am the first and I am the last, and there is no God besides Me"* (Isaiah 44:6). By the way, that is a great verse to bring up with Mormons, who claim that they can become a god. According to their theology, many gods are in the heavens, inhabiting planets with their many wives. Not so, according to the God of the Bible (who happens to know everything). The New Testament affirms monotheism; for example, James 2:19 tells us, *"You believe that God is one. You do well; the demons also believe, and shudder."* According to the Bible, God is one.

There are many places in the Bible where God refers to Himself in the plural. While this does not conclusively prove the doctrine of the Trinity, it certainly does support it. Right from the first chapter of the Bible, we read, *"Let Us make man in Our image, according to Our likeness; and let them rule over the fish of the sea and over the birds of the sky and over the cattle and over all the earth, and over every creeping thing that creeps on the earth"* (Genesis 1:26). Since God is one, who is the "Us"? At the tower of Babel, right before God crashed the party and created the different languages, He said, *"Come, let Us go down and there confuse their language, so that they will not understand one another's speech"* (Genesis 11:7). Again, notice the "Us." Obviously God thinks of Himself in the plural.

Here is an interesting verse from the book of Isaiah, where God is speaking: *"Come near to Me, listen to this: From the first I have not spoken in secret, from the time it took place, I was there. And now the Lord GOD has sent Me, and His Spirit"* (Isaiah 48:16). Feel free to grab a Bible and read the entire chapter to get the context. God is speaking, and according to God, someone He considers to be God sent Him. Interesting, to say the least.

Jesus Is God

I do not know of any group calling itself Christian that does not believe the Father is God. This is one aspect of the Trinity that critics agree on. Jesus Himself instructed people to pray to the Father: *"Our Father who is in heaven, hallowed be Your name"* (Matthew 6:9). We will soon address the reason that Jesus, as God, could direct people to pray to God, but first, let's look at what the Bible says about the deity of Christ. My favorite verses to show the divinity of Christ are John 1, Philippians 2, and John 17. These are excellent passages to show someone that Jesus is God. Each of these passages, discussed below, is wonderful in its own right, but when used together you can make a persuasive case for Christ.

JOHN 1

"In the beginning was the Word, and the Word was with God, and the Word was God. He was in the beginning with God. All things came into being through Him, and apart from Him nothing came into being that has come into being" (John 1:1–3). Here we learn some great things about this one known as "the Word." He existed at the beginning with God, and He was God. In addition, everything that has ever come into existence did so through the Word. That sounds like a description of God! Later in the same chapter, the identity of the Word is clarified: *"And the Word became flesh, and dwelt among us, and we saw His glory, glory as of the only begotten from the Father, full of grace and truth...For the Law was given through Moses; grace and truth were realized through Jesus Christ"* (John 1:14,17). Jesus Christ is the Word who existed before the world began. It's clear that Jesus is referred to as God and He is also shown to be the Creator of all things. Jesus Christ is our Creator God.

PHILIPPIANS 2

The beginning of Philippians 2 is a lesson in humility. Paul is instructing us to love and serve others, beginning with our attitude. He wants us to lay aside our rights and desires in the interest of others. Inspired by the Holy Spirit, Paul uses history's greatest example of humility. In doing so, Paul also reveals the lengths to which Christ went in His service to us:

Have this attitude in yourselves which was also in Christ Jesus, who, although He existed in the form of God, did not regard equality with God a thing to be grasped, but emptied Himself, taking the form of a bond-servant, and being made in the likeness of men. Being found in appearance as a man, He humbled Himself by becoming obedient to the point of death, even death on a cross. For this reason also, God highly exalted Him, and bestowed on Him the name which is above every name, so that at the name of Jesus every knee will bow, of those who are in heaven and on earth and under the earth, and that every tongue will confess that Jesus Christ is Lord, to the glory of God the Father." (Philippians 2:5–11)

The greatest example of humility was when God humbled Himself, took on the form of a man and died on the cross. Jesus, before He was born in Bethlehem, existed in the form of God. Also seen in John 1 and John 17, this is known as the preexistence of Christ, the fact that Jesus is eternal.

At His incarnation, Jesus didn't cease being the eternal God. He has always existed in the form of God, but at the time of His choosing, He *"emptied Himself, taking the form of a bond-servant, and being made in the likeness of men"* (Philippians 2:7). When Jesus took on the form of man, it was the addition of humanity, not the subtraction of deity. He became a humble bondservant, exchanging the outward manifestation of God for the outward manifestation of man. Nowhere does the Bible claim that He transferred His attributes or His nature; rather He clothed Himself with humanity, changing His form, His appearance. This is the key to understanding much about Jesus. If Jesus is God, why didn't He know everything? Why did He get hungry? Why did He claim the Father was greater than Him? All these questions are easily answered when we understand that Jesus humbled Himself or emptied Himself and took the form of a bond-servant.

Theologians have a term for what is described in Philippians 2: "kenosis." Kenosis is defined as Christ's voluntary giving up of the full expression of His divine rights and attributes. Dr. Emery Bancroft said, "Christ voluntarily restricted the use of His divine attributes, limiting their use to His role as a servant. He resigned, not the possession, nor yet entirely the use but rather the independent exercise of the divine attributes."[4] Dr. Chris Mueller put it this way, "Christ restricted the use of His divine attributes so that He could perfectly experience the nature of unglorified humanity. He did not use His power to lift Himself above humanity."[5] As a humble servant, of course, Jesus would do the will of the Father. As one who had taken on human nature, of course, He would pray to the Father. God willingly chose to humble Himself and take the form of a bond-servant, Jesus Christ. *"For you know the grace of our Lord Jesus Christ, that though He was rich, yet for your sake He became poor, so that you through His poverty might become rich"* (2 Corinthians 8:9).

JOHN 17

Another significant evidence of the deity of Jesus is found in His high priestly prayer. As Christ prays to the Father He says, *"Now, Father, glorify Me together with Yourself, with the glory which I had with You before the world was"* (John 17:5). According to Jesus, He was preexistent before the world began. Even more amazing,

---

4   Bancroft, Christian Theology, p. 109.
5   Faith Bible Church Training Center curriculum, 2018, unpublished. Faith Bible Church, Temecula, CA.

Jesus is about to die on the cross and rise from the dead to become reunited with the Father, and He mentions the glory they shared in eternity past! This is astounding! Who shares the glory with the Father? The eternal Son, that's who! The Trinity is one in being and one in glory.

The Holy Spirit Is God

The Holy Spirit is the third person if the Trinity. Like Jesus, the Holy Spirit is God. Some have mistaken the Holy Spirit to be simply a force, a kind of energy. This is incorrect; the Bible clearly presents the Spirit as a person with personal attributes. He teaches, bears witness to Jesus, guides, and intercedes, as seen in the following verses:

"But the Helper, the Holy Spirit...He will teach you all things"
(John 14:26)

"...not in words taught by human wisdom but in those taught by the Spirit" (1 Corinthians 2:13).

"When the Helper comes..., that is the Spirit of truth who proceeds from the Father, He will testify about Me"
(John 15:26)

"Then the Spirit said to Philip, 'Go up and join this chariot'"
(Acts 8:29).

"In the same way the Spirit also helps our weakness;...the Spirit Himself intercedes for us with groanings too deep for words"
(Romans 8:26)

There are not as many references to the deity of the Holy Spirit in the Bible as there are of the Father and Jesus. Maybe this is because the role of the Holy Spirit is to glorify the Son. Maybe the Spirit did not spend much time explaining Himself because He was too busy pointing people to Jesus. Jesus tells us, *"But when He, the Spirit of truth, comes, He will guide you into all the truth; for He will not speak on His own initiative, but whatever He hears, He will speak; and He will disclose to you what is to come. He will glorify Me, for He will take of Mine and will disclose it to you"* (John 16:13,14). Even so, there is enough information about the Holy Spirit for us to understand who He is. Here's a small sampling:

The Holy Spirit is referred to as the Lord—
"Now the Lord is the Spirit, and where the Spirit of the Lord is, there is liberty" (2 Corinthians 3:17)

People are justified in the Spirit—
"but you were justified in the name of the Lord Jesus Christ and in the Spirit of our God" (1 Corinthians 6:11)

Like Jesus, the Holy Spirit was present during creation—
"The earth was formless and void, and darkness was over the surface of the deep, and the Spirit of God was moving over the surface of the waters" (Genesis 1:2)

In Acts 5, we have the sad account of Ananias and Sapphira, a married couple who tried to deceive the church. As Peter confronts Ananias about lying, he reminds him who the Holy Spirit is—

"Ananias, why has Satan filled your heart to lie to the Holy Spirit and to keep back some of the price of the land?...You have not lied to men but to God" (Acts 5:3,4)

The Holy Spirit is God. It's no wonder we are told to baptize believers in His name—

"Go therefore and make disciples of all the nations, baptizing them in the name of the Father and the Son and the Holy Spirit" (Matthew 28:19)

Three in One, or the Sneaky One?

A heresy called "modalism" denies the Trinity, twisting God's nature into something easier for some to grasp. Modern-day modalists are the Oneness Pentecostals or "Jesus Only" churches. They twist the verse we just looked at, Matthew 28:19, and interpret it in a way that is foreign to the Scriptures. They believe the name of the Father, the Son, and the Holy Spirit is Jesus; therefore, we need to baptize in Jesus' name only. They view the three persons of the Trinity as three different manifestations of the same God, who appears in only one "mode" at any time. According to them, when the Father was in heaven, Jesus and the Holy Spirit did not exist, since they are all the same person. When Jesus was walking the earth, the Father did not exist in heaven. When the Holy Spirit is at work, the Father and the Son are nowhere to be found, since (according to their unbiblical teaching) they are all the same person. It's as if God wears different masks, depending on what He wants to do.

It's sneaky and deceptive, if you ask me. Modalism is not biblical since there are places in the Bible where the three members of the Trinity are involved at the same time. The baptism of Jesus is one such place: *"After being baptized, Jesus came up immediately from the water; and behold, the heavens were opened, and he saw the Spirit of God descending as a dove and lighting on Him, and behold, a voice out of the heavens said, 'This is My beloved Son, in whom I am well-pleased'"* (Matthew 3:16,17). The Father is not the Son, the Son is not the Spirit, and the Spirit is not the Father. They are three separate persons who exist within the same being. They function differently, mainly because they have different roles.

Many apologetic questions about the members of the Trinity can be understood in light of their differing roles. We have already seen the Son's role as a bond-servant who died on the cross for our sin, and the Holy Spirit's role as the One who glorifies the Son. The difference in function is not the same as the difference in being. Men and women are both human beings, but they have different roles, according to Scripture: *"But I want you to understand that Christ is the head of every man, and the man is the head of a woman, and God is the head of Christ"* (1 Corinthians 11:3). God the Father is the head of Christ. They have differing roles, and as we have seen throughout this chapter on apologetics, they are both persons of the Trinity.

Never Stop Learning

Many great, in-depth books have been written on the Trinity. Some are listed in the bibliography section; please add them to your reading list. It's so important to have a biblical understanding of this important doctrine. As long as there are enemies of the gospel, there will be Scripture twisters and deceivers. I encourage you to be an apologist: one who is ready to make a defense for the hope that is within you. Never stop studying your Bible. It's your sword, and the more you use it, the better your defense will be.

Most important, don't forget the place of apologetics. It's not the end; it's a means to an end. The end is the gospel—our goal is to reach unbelievers with the message of salvation. It's not enough to show someone why the Trinity is true; we need to present the gospel so they can be saved. It is the *gospel* that is *"the power of God for salvation"* (Romans 1:16). Apologetics simply clears the way for evangelism.

QUESTIONS FOR REFLECTION

1. How much do you need to know in order to witness? Is it okay to wait until you feel you have every answer? Why or why not?

2. Read 1 Corinthians 2:14. Why is it difficult for an unbeliever to understand spiritual things?

3. When people say we shouldn't use the Bible because they don't believe it, how should we respond and why?

4. According to Romans 1:18–25, will not believing in God be a valid excuse on Judgment Day? Based on these verses, is anyone truly an atheist or agnostic? Explain.

5. When thinking of the Trinity, why is it important to understand that God is incomprehensible?

6. How could you define the Trinity, explaining some of the biblical truths about God's triune nature?

7. What are some verses showing that Jesus and the Holy Spirit are God?

8. What role should apologetics play in our evangelism? Why is this?

WATCH THIS!

- Go to eddieroman.com and click Watch on the top menu.
- Watch the video labeled "Answering Skeptics."
- Stand your ground, answer questions, and get to the gospel.

PRAYER POINT

- Pray that God would help you to defend the faith as you evangelize the lost.

5

ON THE
BATTLEFIELD

When we think about the Christian life, we like to think about the good parts: fellowship, worship, encouraging Bible studies, and the warm feelings we receive from the realization that our Creator loves us. These are a few benefits of walking with the Lord, yet the believer's walk is not all blessings and joy. When meditating on the promises of God, how often do we think of suffering? If you are a Christian, you will suffer—that's a promise from God: *"Indeed, all who desire to live godly in Christ Jesus will be persecuted"* (2 Timothy 3:12). Did you catch that? "All" Christians will encounter suffering and persecution. Paul, under the inspiration of the Holy Spirit, made that statement while instructing Timothy to persevere in the midst of opposition while advancing the gospel.

Listen to Paul as he gives an overview of the things he endured as a result of his Christian walk:

Five times I received from the Jews thirty-nine lashes. Three times I was beaten with rods, once I was stoned, three times I was shipwrecked, a night and a day I have spent in the deep. I have been on frequent journeys, in dangers from rivers, dangers from robbers, dangers from my countrymen, dangers from the Gentiles, dangers in the city, dangers in the wilderness, dangers on the sea, dangers among false brethren; I have been in labor and hardship, through many sleepless nights, in hunger and thirst, often without food, in cold and exposure. Apart from such external things, there is the daily pressure on me of concern for all the churches.

(2 Corinthians 11:24–28)

I seriously doubt Paul had a smile on his face as he went through all of that. His life was no relaxing men's retreat. Suffering is an expected part of the life of every believer, as Paul makes clear: *"The Spirit Himself testifies with our spirit that we are children of God, and if children, heirs also, heirs of God and fellow heirs with Christ, if indeed we suffer with Him so that we may also be glorified with Him. For I consider that the sufferings of this present time are not worthy to be compared with the glory that is to be revealed to us"* (Romans 8:16–18). Heaven is our hope; our eternal home will be fantastic and pain-free. One day all believers will be glorified and, like the Lego guy, we'll be able to say, "Everything is awesome!" However, it's important to remember we're not there yet. Everything is not awesome in a world where enemies of God challenge His Word and direct their hatred for Him at His children.

Don't Run from the Blessing

Rather than running away from the pain that will come from living for Christ, it's a good idea to understand and embrace it.

> *I count all things to be loss in view of the surpassing value of knowing Christ Jesus my Lord, for whom I have suffered the loss of all things, and count them but rubbish so that I may gain Christ, and may be found in Him, not having a righteousness of my own derived from the Law, but that which is through faith in Christ, the righteousness which comes from God on the basis of faith, that I may know Him and the power of His resurrection and the fellowship of His sufferings, being conformed to His death.* (Philippians 3:8–10)

When you are persecuted or endure hardship for the sake of the gospel, remember that knowing Christ is worth it. It's worth *so much more!* I'm not sure we will ever fully comprehend what our relationship with Jesus Christ is worth. We do not suffer because we are salesmen, selling a cheap product which people are tired of hearing about. We suffer for promoting someone we know: the living, all-powerful, eternal, all-knowing, sovereign Creator God, and His enemies hate us. Don't let them stop you from proclaiming His name. Although suffering for Christ is not fun, God promises to use it for our benefit.

When we accept that suffering is a normal part of the Christian life, we should not be shocked when we endure hardship for the gospel, as Peter reminds us: *"Beloved, do not be surprised at the fiery ordeal among you, which comes upon you for your testing, as though some strange thing were happening to you; but to the degree that you share the sufferings of Christ, keep on rejoicing, so that also at the revelation of His glory you may rejoice with exultation"* (1 Peter 4:12,13).

The pain endured by Christians never goes to waste. God uses all things for His purposes. *"And we know that God causes all things to work together for good to those who love God, to those who are called according to His purpose. For those whom He foreknew, He also predestined to become conformed to the image of His Son, so that He would be the firstborn among many brethren"* (Romans 8:28,29). When the Father uses persecution to conform you into the image of His Son, it's a good thing. When the outcome of a trial, including the trial of evangelism, produces greater endurance, praise the Lord! Consider this encouragement from James: *"Consider it all joy, my brethren, when you encounter various trials, knowing that the testing of your faith produces endurance. And let endurance have its perfect result, so that you may be perfect and complete, lacking in nothing"* (James 1:2–4).

Even better yet, follow the example of Peter and the apostles. When they refused to stop preaching the gospel, the Jewish leaders threw them in jail, *"flogged them and ordered them not to speak in the name of Jesus, and then released them. So they went on their way from the presence of the Council, rejoicing that they had been considered worthy to suffer shame for His name. And every day, in the temple and from house to house, they kept right on teaching and preaching Jesus as the Christ"* (Acts 5:40–42). The apostles rejoiced after suffering for Christ! Why? Was it because they love pain? Were they thrilled that the flogging would give them honor among other evangelists? No way; they rejoiced because they were counted "worthy"! Their association with Christ and incessant proclamation of His name made them worthy of persecution.

Worthy to Suffer

Many people seek a title or position in the church to identify their worthiness. From God's perspective, it is those who suffer for Christ who are worthy. In fact, God seems to have a special place for those who have suffered the most for the cause of Christ:

> When the Lamb broke the fifth seal, I saw underneath the altar the souls of those who had been slain because of the word of God, and because of the testimony which they had maintained; and they cried out with a loud voice, saying, "How long, O Lord, holy and true, will You refrain from judging and avenging our blood on those who dwell on the earth?" And there was given to each of them a white robe; and they were told that they should rest for a little while longer, until the number of their fellow servants and their brethren who were to be killed even as they had been, would be completed also. (Revelation 6:9–11)

There are so many incredible things about that passage of Scripture. Notice how the martyrs want justice: *"How long, O Lord, holy and true, will You refrain from judging and avenging our blood on those who dwell on the earth?"* (Revelation 6:10). It's natural to want to be treated fairly, especially when you've done nothing wrong. In 2016, Mike Stockwell, leader of the ministry Cross Country Evangelism, faced a day in court in England for street preaching. Mike leads evangelism outreaches, mainly by open-air preaching. The UK has "hate speech" laws that have been applied to Christians who have publicly proclaimed Romans 1 and other sections of Scripture that tell the truth about the sin of homosexuality.

Christian Concern, an organization that tracks Christian persecution, provided the following coverage of Mike Stockwell's trial:

> Michael Overd, Adrian Clark, Michael Stockwell and another
> friend were preaching in a Bristol shopping area last July.
> They took it in turns to speak, and to respond to questions,
> objections and abuse from the crowd that gathered. The men
> explained the difference between Islam and Christianity,
> using the Bible and references to the Qur'an. They spoke of
> God's love, and the uniqueness of Jesus Christ. After about
> an hour, however, Mr Overd's preaching was interrupted
> by a police officer. He was then forcibly removed from the
> scene by the officer.
>
> Video evidence from Mr Overd's bodycam shows him falling
> to the floor and crying out in pain. The video also records
> the police officer saying that Mr Overd was "challenging
> homophobia" and "challenging Muslims", to which Mr
> Overd responds that he and his friends were "just saying
> what the Bible says".[6]

Prosecutor Ian Jackson told the court that, "Although the
words preached are included in a version of the Bible in 1611,
this does not mean that they are incapable of amounting to a
public order offence in 2016."[7] The prosecutor also argued, "To
say to someone that Jesus is the only God is not a matter of truth.
To the extent that they are saying that the only way to God is
through Jesus, that cannot be a truth."[8]

---

6 "Christian preachers stand trial in Bristol," Christian Concern, February
   22, 2017 <tinyurl.com/yaf23mfo>.
7 "Street preachers who quoted Bible, convicted in 'modern-day heresy
   trial,'" Christian Concern, February 28, 2017 <tinyurl.com/ycvcmlj6>.
8 Ibid.

Mike Stockwell and Mike Overd were found guilty of "public disorder and religiously aggravated speech." Between court costs and fines, they were ordered to pay approximately $3,000 each. This case is personal to me because Mike Stockwell is a friend. I've open-air preached alongside Mike, and he has stayed at my home; he's a committed evangelist and a man of integrity. The preachers broke no laws. The verdict was based on the following quote from Chief Inspector Andy Williams: "The police have to strike the balance between the right to freedom of expression and free speech and behavior that causes a member of the public to feel harassed, alarmed or distressed as a result of what is said or done."[9]

In this case, the homosexuals and Muslims "felt harassed" when the men quoted verses confronting the sins of homosexuality and idolatry. We live in a world where feelings are considered more important than the truth of the gospel. These laws may not be in place here in America, but I suspect they are coming soon. In any case, the same worldly mindset is already here. We must press on in the face of this opposition. Mike was discouraged when the verdict came, but it did not stop him. He continues to open-air preach because he understands that persecution and opposition are part of the Christian's job description. In eternity Mike will not regret his days on earth. True servants of the Most High God press on, serving Him regardless of the cost.

Another sobering truth of Revelation 6 is that Christians will suffer until the end, *"until the number of their fellow servants and their brethren who were to be killed even as they had been, would be completed also"* (Revelation 6:11). While this is not a study on martyrdom, the general principle is that Christians suffer for a

---

9   "Christian street preachers fined over Bristol shopping centre sermon," BBC News, March 1, 2017 <tinyurl.com/y7xll94t>.

reason. We may not always know or understand the reason, but God does, and we should take comfort in that.

While much hardship faced by Christians is for a good reason, sometimes it's not. Sometimes we bring unnecessary trouble upon ourselves for the wrong reasons. If you suffer because you are obnoxious, rude, or mean, that is not suffering for Christ; it's suffering for dumbness. It is dumb to tell a homosexual that God created "Adam and Eve, not Adam and Steve." Why in the world would a homosexual, who is already in defensive mode against you, think that is funny? I once watched as a Christian said that to a homosexual he had just met, and it did not go well. If you suffer for saying unkind things, please don't tell anyone you are persecuted for Christ. It's okay to suffer for Christ; it's not okay to suffer for lack of wisdom. I've seen "Jesus saves" illegally spray-painted on a wall. If the painter were caught and fined, that wouldn't be persecution; it would be justice. *"If you are reviled for the name of Christ, you are blessed, because the Spirit of glory and of God rests on you. Make sure that none of you suffers as a murderer, or thief, or evildoer, or a troublesome meddler"* (1 Peter 4:14,15).

Truth in Advertising

Because suffering is an expected part of life, especially for Christians, it's important to be truthful when presenting the gospel. In our excitement and longing to see others come to Jesus, it's possible for us to offer a "too good to be true" gospel message. Some Christians use the benefits of salvation to draw others to Christ in their evangelism. They say things like, "Come to Christ; you'll be happy. Give your life to Christ; He will fix your marriage." Those things may be true at times, but using possible blessings that may come from God as a drawing card for evangelism creates problems. First, you shouldn't make promises that are not certain. For example, God may fix a marriage once an evil husband is redeemed, but He may not. What if the wife has had enough and decides to leave, in spite of the husband's changed life? God doesn't promise Christians a perfectly smooth and happy life—in fact, as we've read, it's just the opposite.

Many people will suffer as a direct result of their conversion. Mormons, Jehovah's Witnesses, and many other cultic groups encourage their adherents to ostracize and shame those who leave. Muslims are known worldwide for their harsh treatment of those who convert to Christianity. Being cut off from a loving family is the price many pay for following Christ; countless others pay the ultimate price and are killed for their faith. As you evangelize, don't give the impression that coming to Christ will solve all problems. In many cases, coming to Christ will create problems. These problems may be a result of sin, but they are problems nonetheless. To give the impression that Christians live happily ever after during this life is false advertising.

I'm not sure where the idea came from that Christianity is all joy and happiness, but it sure wasn't the Bible. Read the book of Acts; there's no way you can escape the fact that the first Christians were persecuted repeatedly. In Paul's case, God even prepared him for the suffering that was to come. When Ananias was hesitant to assist Paul after his conversion, God said to Ananias, *"Go, for he is a chosen instrument of Mine, to bear My name before the Gentiles and kings and the sons of Israel; for I will show him how much he must suffer for My name's sake"* (Acts 9:15,16). Most of us will not suffer as the apostle Paul did, and I'm thankful; yet as we step out and share the good news of Jesus Christ, many will hate us for it. Jesus said, *"If the world hates you, you know that it has hated Me before it hated you"* (John 15:18).

Ready for Battle

In light of all the hatred and persecution directed at Christ's servants, isn't it easier to just lay low and keep your mouth shut? Maybe, but it's not right. It is neither right nor acceptable for a servant of the Lord to cower when it comes to evangelism. In the military, going AWOL (absent without leave) is a serious offense. How much more severe is going AWOL from our duty in the battle for souls? Rather than flee the battle, we should heed Paul's advice to Timothy: *"Suffer hardship with me, as a good soldier of Christ Jesus. No soldier in active service entangles himself in the affairs of everyday life, so that he may please the one who enlisted him as a soldier"* (2 Timothy 2:3,4).

Instead of hiding from the battle or pretending it doesn't exist, as soldiers of Christ we need to be ready. Ephesians 6, known as the "spiritual warfare" chapter, has much that applies as we battle for the lost. For the remainder of this chapter, we are going to go verse by verse through this sobering passage, considering what it says about evangelism:

> *Finally, be strong in the Lord and in the strength of His might. Put on the full armor of God, so that you will be able to stand firm against the schemes of the devil. For our struggle is not against flesh and blood, but against the rulers, against the powers, against the world forces of this darkness, against the spiritual forces of wickedness in the heavenly places. Therefore,*

take up the full armor of God, so that you will be able to resist in the evil day, and having done everything, to stand firm. Stand firm therefore, having girded your loins with truth, and having put on the breastplate of righteousness, and having shod your feet with the preparation of the gospel of peace; in addition to all, taking up the shield of faith with which you will be able to extinguish all the flaming arrows of the evil one. And take the helmet of salvation, and the sword of the Spirit, which is the word of God.

With all prayer and petition pray at all times in the Spirit, and with this in view, be on the alert with all perseverance and petition for all the saints, and pray on my behalf, that utterance may be given to me in the opening of my mouth, to make known with boldness the mystery of the gospel, for which I am an ambassador in chains; that in proclaiming it I may speak boldly, as I ought to speak."   (Ephesians 6:10–20)

WHOSE MIGHT IS IT?

The passage opens with a fundamental principle concerning evangelism, as well as pretty much everything else we do as Christians: *"Be strong in the Lord and in the strength of His might"* (Ephesians 6:10). Many people have the false perception that evangelism is for tough guys, those who have the nerve to go against the grain and face opposition. What we fail to realize is, this view puts our faith in the flesh. Tough guys do not seek God's help; they tough it out on their own. We are not called to be strong in our flesh, but *"in the Lord and in the strength of His might."* We should not be trusting in our might or depending on our intellect. When I approach someone I intend to witness to,

I usually pray something like this: "Father, I have no idea what is about to happen. This person might be way smarter than me, he may outwit me, and he could get angry. I ask you to guide me through this, help me to present the gospel clearly in a way that he can understand. Please save him."

Apologetics are important, but you must be cautious when applying your arguments, remembering that *"it is the Spirit who gives life; the flesh profits nothing"* (John 6:63). Great intellects are a blessing from God, but if you tend to rely heavily on your apologetical abilities instead of trusting in the Lord, beware. Humans don't stand much of a chance against the evil spirits we are waging war against. A proud evangelist is a useless one.

PUT IT ON

"Put on the full armor of God, so that you will be able to stand firm against the schemes of the devil" (Ephesians 6:11). The word "put" is an imperative, meaning it is not a suggestion but a command. We must depend on God as we reach out to the lost since the devil and his demonic coworkers will scheme against us. They may influence people to oppose, challenge, ridicule, and shame us. For the sake of the lost and the glory of God, we must stand firm. We can do this only by depending wholly on Christ.

DEMONIC REALITY

"For our struggle is not against flesh and blood, but against the rulers, against the powers, against the world forces of this darkness, against the spiritual forces of wickedness in the heavenly places" (Ephesians 6:12). This verse is both terrifying and assuring. The realization that the invisible demonic realm is actively working against us is horrifying. Maybe you're not the kind of Christian who thinks

much about fallen angels. Many believers rightfully reject false demonic claims, such as "the devil made me do it," or blaming a "spirit of lust" as the cause of personal sin. In rejecting these claims, many go too far and dismiss the spiritual realm altogether. Let us never forget that the Bible is clear, demons exist and they war against the gospel. The more you try to reason with the lost about seemingly clear matters, the more you will understand that something unworldly and evil is influencing unbelievers.

The recent "transgender" debacle is a good example. Retailers and colleges nationwide are insisting that men and women use the bathroom of their choice, guided only by the gender they "self-identify" as. This is in a nation where registered sex offenders live in every neighborhood. According to the Department of Justice, an American was sexually assaulted every 98 seconds in 2015.[10] Taking male and female distinctions away from public restrooms and locker rooms is sure to spell disaster. Imagine grown men near young women and girls in a room where both are exposed or naked. Unfortunately, we no longer need to imagine, for this is standard practice in many schools and businesses. This is not due to a shortage of restrooms or any other logical reason. I believe it is demonic, either instigated by Satan or demonically inspired. God's Word reminds us, *"We know that we are of God, and that the whole world lies in the power of the evil one"* (1 John 5:19).

DEMONS HATE JESUS

I have seen rational men and women become livid with anger at the mere mention of Jesus. I was once explaining the gospel to a young lady outside of a mall in Anaheim. A man in a business

---

10 Department of Justice, Office of Justice Programs, Bureau of Justice Statistics, National Crime Victimization Survey, 2010–2014 (2015).

suit happened to be listening in, and suddenly his face became beet red and he exploded, shouting curses at me. It was wild; he went from zero to rage in seconds. I've never seen anything like it since (praise the Lord). Gospel talk will bring demonic activity to your doorstep. This is why we must personalize the directives of Ephesians 6: *"Therefore, take up the full armor of God, so that you will be able to resist in the evil day, and having done everything, to stand firm. Stand firm therefore, having girded your loins with truth..."* (Ephesians 6:13,14).

At first glance, this mention of "truth" seems to be the Word of God. However, the Word is introduced later in this section. "Truth" in this passage refers to truthfulness, integrity. The enemy will use lies and deception to fight against the gospel and righteousness. This week on Facebook, an unbeliever "friend" (someone I don't know who responded to a comment on one of my posts) mocked the notion that only two genders exist. He asserted that male and female are only two of the fifty-two genders in existence, citing Wikipedia as a reference. His confidence and boldness in his statement were notable, but regardless of his presentation, he was wrong. Fifty-two genders? What a ridiculous lie. Maybe he knows it's a lie or maybe he's deceived himself. In either case, he speaks lies. Society may create its definitions of whatever it wants, and many may believe it, but lies remain lies.

As you enter into gospel discussions on enemy territory, speak the truth; do not agree with lies. When I talk with Mormons, I point out that their version of Jesus is not the real Jesus, but a counterfeit invented by Mormon leadership. I would never want a cult member to think we are somehow "brothers" in a Christian sense. We may be brothers in humanity, but those who lie about my Lord are not my spiritual brothers. Be sure to walk in truth.

THE RIGHTEOUSNESS OF CHRIST

Paul continues that we are to stand firm, *"having put on the breastplate of righteousness"* (Ephesians 6:14). Character attacks against Christians are commonplace during evangelism. As you draw attention to people's sin, they will attempt to draw attention to yours. You will be accused of thinking yourself to be better than those you evangelize. "You think you're better than me? Are you perfect?" Agree with the unbeliever that you are not perfect, but nevertheless, you have righteousness. Then explain where your righteousness came from—it was a gift from the Lord Jesus.

BE PREPARED

"Having shod your feet with the preparation of the gospel of peace" (Ephesians 6:15). One of the main excuses I hear from Christians who don't share their faith is that they just don't know what to say. If you feel as if you wouldn't know how to preach the gospel to an unbeliever, my question is this: how much time and effort have you put into your gospel presentation? Have you worked on your preparation of the gospel of peace? One of the saddest things I encounter on the street is Christians who cannot explain the gospel. If that describes you, study and make the effort to prepare yourself. It's not difficult; it simply takes time. Most Christians understand the gospel, but understanding what it is and knowing how to present it are two different things.

Some Christians learn by trial and error. They zealously jump into evangelism, trying every method and eventually figuring out what seems to work. I don't have a problem with that; I would much rather see weak attempts at evangelism than no attempts at all. Each Christian must start somewhere. Believers are at different levels of maturity and knowledge, so unless someone is involved in outright sin during their evangelism efforts, we shouldn't discourage them. I've heard Christians mocking street evangelists for holding up a cross or a sign in a public place, and I have to wonder whose side the mockers are on. If we are more concerned with our image or remaining "cool" (whatever that happens to mean at the moment) than we are with reaching the lost, I think a heart check is in order. Often those criticizing the public evangelism efforts of others are not involved in evangelism at all. Instead of criticizing, we can be encouraged by the zeal of others.

FAITH

"In addition to all, taking up the shield of faith with which you will be able to extinguish all the flaming arrows of the evil one" (Ephesians 6:16). When our Scripture memory, intellect, strategy, method, and wit fails, faith keeps us going: *"Now faith is the assurance of things hoped for, the conviction of things not seen"* (Hebrews 11:1). We can advance without fear because we trust God. We will not have answers to every question, we will not know how to deal with every circumstance we face, but by faith, we can trust God and press on.

Atheists will never stop coming up with ways to attack Christ and His Word. Disheartening images of Christians having their heads chopped off by ISIS or some other group will probably continue until Jesus comes back. The flaming arrows of the enemy keep coming, so we must live by faith. Living by faith is what we are calling men and women to do when we proclaim the gospel, as Paul explains: *"For I am not ashamed of the gospel, for it is the power of God for salvation to everyone who believes, to the Jew first and also to the Greek. For in it the righteousness of God is revealed from faith to faith; as it is written, 'But the righteous man shall live by faith'"* (Romans 1:16,17). As we challenge unbelievers to live by faith, let's not forget to live that way ourselves: *"for we walk by faith, not by sight"* (2 Corinthians 5:7).

CRASH HELMET FOR CHRIST

"And take the helmet of salvation..." (Ephesians 6:17). As we work our way through the spiritual warfare chapter, looking at the various pieces of armor, salvation is likened to a helmet. In my BMX days, most of the guys riding trails didn't wear helmets because they were not considered cool. Only paid pros or nerd kids wore helmets. Helmets get hot, they impair a tiny portion of your vision, and many kids just can't afford the expense. Of course, they can also prevent brain damage and save your life, but most kids aren't thinking of that. Every once in a while someone would want to try a crazy stunt that involved jumping over a car or riding off a roof. In these moments of backyard glory, helmets were acceptable. For super-stunts, even the most hardcore rebel BMXer would ask to borrow a helmet, because every kid knows, you can try anything dangerous if you're wearing a helmet. You might get bruised or even break a leg, but if you have a helmet, you'll live.

Evangelism can be dangerous, but we shouldn't worry because we have a helmet; nothing can destroy our salvation. With that in mind, let's look at a worst possible scenario: martyrdom. I have no desire to die by the sharp blade of ISIS, but if I do, it's not a big deal. I have been saved, redeemed by Jesus Christ, so I will go straight to heaven when I die. As much as I do not want my death to hurt, after the dying is done it will not matter. If my death involves torture I will probably cry out, but look at the big picture. Once we're in the presence of our incredible God and see our Savior face to face, no one is going to care about the way they died. Because of the helmet of salvation we can approach evangelism without fear. When all is said and done, we will be okay. In fact, we will be far more than just okay!

THE POWER OF THE WORD

"And take...the sword of the Spirit, which is the word of God" (Ephesians 6:17). We looked at the Good Person Test, and it's a useful tool, but the best way to prepare for evangelism and apologetics is to read and memorize the Word of God. This is your sword, your defensive and offensive weapon for the spiritual warfare that accompanies every gospel presentation. As you take a person through the Good Person Test, conversations will inevitably go into every different subject possible, so you need to be ready with the Word. The more Scripture you know, the better you will be able to answer questions and explain the truth. During evangelism, I have counseled people on marriage, drug use, alcohol addiction, depression, and many other issues, all with the Word as my guide. God will use you to the extent to which you know His Word.

There is myth within the church that says you don't need to study; the Holy Spirit will show you what to say when you evangelize. It's based on these verses: *"When they bring you before the synagogues and the rulers and the authorities, do not worry about how or what you are to speak in your defense, or what you are to say; for the Holy Spirit will teach you in that very hour what you ought to say"* (Luke 12:11,12). As always, context is everything. Luke 12 is dealing with fear, being afraid when you are forced to stand for your faith, as Jesus makes clear: *"I say to you, My friends, do not be afraid of those who kill the body and after that have no more that they can do...I say to you, everyone who confesses Me before men, the Son of Man will confess him also before the angels of God; but he who denies Me before men will be denied before the angels of God"* (Luke 12:4,8,9). We are to trust God in times of testing and persecution. These verses have nothing to do with our study of the Word. The thought that we don't need to apply ourselves to learn the Bible is ridiculous, in fact, we are told quite the opposite: *"Be diligent to present yourself approved to God as a workman who does not need to be ashamed, accurately handling the word of truth"* (2 Timothy 2:15). Study the Bible as much as you can; you will need it for evangelism—as well as for yourself.

PRAY WITHOUT CEASING

The passage on spiritual warfare closes with an emphasis on prayer. *"With all prayer and petition pray at all times in the Spirit, and with this in view, be on the alert with all perseverance and petition for all the saints, and pray on my behalf, that utterance may be given to me in the opening of my mouth, to make known with boldness the mystery of the gospel"* (Ephesians 6:18,19). In any war, communication is vital. Those on the battlefield must be in constant contact with their commander who leads the battle. As we fight on the front-lines of evangelism, prayer is our open line to God. Gospel conversations can be challenging, requiring us to seek wisdom from God: *"But if any of you lacks wisdom, let him ask of God, who gives to all generously and without reproach, and it will be given to him"* (James 1:5).

Prayer is vital to the gospel presentation, on several fronts. First, we should be praying for more believers to labor in evangelism, as Jesus commanded us: *"The harvest is plentiful, but the laborers are few; therefore beseech the Lord of the harvest to send out laborers into His harvest"* (Luke 10:2). Second, pray that the Word would spread among the lost: *"pray for us that the word of the Lord will spread rapidly and be glorified, just as it did also with you"* (2 Thessalonians 3:1). And third, we should pray for opportunities and boldness to speak about Christ: *"that utterance may be given to me in the opening of my mouth, to make known with boldness the mystery of the gospel"* (Ephesians 6:19). Without prayer, we fight alone. Without Christ's help, we labor in vain, but with God, all things are possible. Conversations with unbelievers can be taxing on your knowledge and patience. Add to that the spiritual nature of it all, and it's easy to see why prayer is essential every moment of every day: *"Pray without ceasing"* (1 Thessalonians 5:17).

Real Life

Having a realistic view of our existence is important. From God's perspective, our brief lives are lived on a battlefield for souls where eternity is at stake. The idea that the Christian life should be a string of happy, joyful experiences is unbiblical. Christians will suffer persecution and opposition because we live in a fallen world and God's enemy is our enemy. Prepare yourself for battle.

QUESTIONS FOR REFLECTION

1. When God saves a person, does He promise to fix every marital issue, financial problem, and make all their dreams

come true? Why is it unrealistic and unbiblical to think the Christian life should be pain-free and easy? _____

_____

_____

2. Read 2 Timothy 3:12 and 1 Peter 4:12,13. Should we expect suffering to be part of our life? If so, why? _____

_____

_____

3. If you are not facing any persecution for your faith, what might that imply about your walk with Christ? _____

_____

_____

4. When the disciples faced persecution and trials, what attitude did they have in response? How does that compare to your response to persecution? _____

_____

_____

_____

5. According to 1 Peter 4:14, is suffering for Christ a blessing or a curse? _____

_____

_____

6. What are some ways we can bring suffering on ourselves by our wrong behavior? _____

_____

_____

7. Consider 2 Timothy 2:3,4. Do you avoid hardship, or are you willing to suffer for Christ? If you have gone spiritually AWOL, what can you do to get back into the battle? _____

_____

_____

_____

8. List the pieces of spiritual armor found in Ephesians 6 and how they relate to evangelism. _____

_____

_____

WATCH THIS!

- Go to eddieroman.com and click Watch on the top menu.
- Watch the video labeled "Tears of the Saints."
- Across the world and across the street, unbelievers need the gospel.

PRAYER POINT

- Pray through Ephesians 6:10–20, asking God to keep His spiritual armor on your mind as you engage in evangelism.

6

GO INTO THE WORLD

In this final chapter, I'm going to encourage you to go for it. Get outside of your comfort zone; talk to lost people. If you mess up (and you will), figure out what you could have done better, pray about it, study the issue and do it again. Find another unbeliever and go for round two. I'm on round three thousand or so, and I still run into difficulties. As soldiers of Christ, we should expect challenges. Obedience in evangelism, hardships included, is better than disobedience in evangelism. The only time we fail

> Obedience in evangelism,
> hardships included, is better than
> disobedience in evangelism.

in evangelism is when we fail to evangelize. Is Christ not worth our very best effort? Is He not worth our blood, sweat, tears, and fears? Evangelism can be scary, but is Christ not worth the occasional concerns we face as we rescue souls from hell?

> Evangelism can be scary, but is Christ not worth the occasional concerns we face as we rescue souls from hell?

Firefighters

When I was a kid, I was bike riding in my neighborhood and saw a fire in a dry canyon. I rolled up to the curb next to a fire truck as the men were putting on their jackets and helmets. White smoke was billowing out of the canyon, and the heat was nearly unbearable. The firemen grabbed a hose, formed a line, ran down into the canyon and disappeared into the smoke. This was pretty much the most radical thing I'd ever seen. I was in awe of these seemingly fearless men—they were my new heroes, better than Spider-Man! I wondered, "Who in the world is crazy enough to do that?"

Today I'm older, wiser, and still afraid to run into canyon fires. If there is a fire in your house, don't call me because I'm not a fireman. Since that day on the canyon rim, I've come to understand that firemen are not crazy. Some may begin their career with a reckless mindset, but that quickly dissipates with maturity and discipline. If you have any firefighter friends, you know they are rational human beings. They eat, sleep, and get injured just like everyone else. Some have bold and daring personalities, while others are cautious and safe. Firemen are not insane, but they do have three things most people do not have, and because of this, they go into burning buildings.

Firemen can do things the rest of us can't do because they have firefighting training, fire gear, and firefighting experience. It is that simple. If you had those things, you too could enter a smoke-filled room to rescue those in danger. There is not a firefighter gene or a firefighter gift of the Spirit. These brave men and women have dedicated themselves to acquiring the necessary training, gear, and experience. The reason many Christians are not comfortable evangelizing is that they lack those three essential things. If you take the time to gain all three, evangelism will become a regular part of your life. Let's take a look at each one.

Training

We live in a world of information. Anyone with a computer or smart phone can Google the instructions needed to do almost anything. You can learn and in many cases view step-by-step videos of how to fix a car engine, build a rocket, or master quantum mechanics. You can also watch people evangelize the lost and engage in apologetic debates. In my opinion, Ray Comfort is the king of Internet witnessing. Watching him witness to people (as he films his conversations with his phone) is an invaluable training resource.[11] Listening to the conversations is only part of the value; we can learn much from Ray's respect and genuine

---

11 You can find Ray's videos and other evangelism training materials at livingwaters.com.

concern for the people he talks with. How many of us would be willing to speak kindly to a man dressed as a woman as he belittles us? Watching Ray is a lesson in patience and graciousness. His one-on-one witnessing is an example of how a Christian should gently and respectfully speak with an unbeliever, as we're commanded to do: *"to malign no one, to be peaceable, gentle, showing every consideration for all men."* (Titus 3:2).

The easiest way to learn how to witness is to watch someone else evangelizing, live and in person. If your church has an evangelism team, ask to tag along. I watched people hand out tracts and witness to strangers long before I tried it myself. I now lead teams on local outreaches, and having new Christians come along is always a blessing. Once nervous Christians come to watch and see how simple and natural it is, they feel much more confident to join the conversation. Just this morning I visited a local junior college with three people from my church, who had come to witness to students for the first time. None of the three had witnessed to strangers before. I gave them a few quick suggestions, and we found an area where the students congregate in between classes. I began speaking to three guys, and after a while, I looked over, and one of the women from my church was witnessing to a young lady. During the ninety minutes we visited, all three had gospel conversations with students. They had stepped out in faith, and God used them to explain His message of salvation to unbelievers! They were so encouraged.

If your church is not involved in street witnessing but does go door to door, join them! Evangelism happens in many different ways; the settings change, but the message is what matters. Learn from those at your church who are actively witnessing. Many churches do not have an organized evangelism outreach, yet there may be men and women serving at the church who witness on their own without any fanfare. Ask around; God may have a faithful evangelist in your congregation.

In addition to churches, there are ministries that offer training. The Living Waters training seminar that gave me my start, the Ambassadors' Academy, is still going strong in California.[12] Sports Fan Outreach is a ministry that holds outreaches at major sports events across America.[13] Their annual Super Bowl Outreach is an amazing time of training and fellowship for street preachers from across the nation. Striving For Eternity, led by Andrew Rappaport, holds seminars and evangelism training at churches nationwide.[14] It may be expensive to travel to another state for a training weekend, but if you believe God has called you to evangelize, it's something to consider. It could change your life.

One man who changed my life is a sidewalk saint named John Barros. A member of St. Andrew's Chapel near Orlando, John has been standing on the sidewalk outside an abortion clinic nearly every weekday for over six years. He faithfully calls people to repent and forsake their scheduled abortion. It is one of the most heart-wrenching ministries I've seen. Hard-hearted, self-focused women and men ignore John's pleas day after day. Sometimes they laugh or curse at him as they keep the appointment for the murder of their unborn child. It's such a brutal environment to step into, as angry boyfriends, security guards, horrible parents, and murder-minded women direct their anger at John. C. T. Studd once said, "Some want to live within the sound of church

---

12 For Living Waters evangelism training, go to ambassadorsacademy.com.
13 For Sports Fan Outreach, go to sfoi.org.
14 For Striving For Eternity, go to strivingforeternity.org

or chapel bell; I want to run a rescue shop, within a yard of hell." John Barros has found that rescue shop, and he runs it very well. On average, John is used by the Lord to turn one pregnant mother away from abortion each day. In addition, many have trusted Christ as a result of their interaction with him.

I had the opportunity to spend three days with John, and the experience shaped the way I think about abortion ministry and motivated me to minister at abortion clinics in my area. On my third visit to a clinic in San Diego, I walked with a couple from their car to the clinic door, gently asking them to turn away. In a normal tone of voice, I told them God created their child, and He will judge their sin of murder. I told them to listen to their conscience and that if they don't, their guilt and shame will follow them for the rest of their lives. Then I explained the gospel and God's mercy toward repentant people. The conversation lasted about two minutes. They entered the abortion clinic. I was discouraged. Five minutes later, the clinic door opened, they exited, got back in their car and left. She changed her mind—she decided not to go through with the abortion! A life was saved and the gospel had been given. The clinic workers were livid, and I was rejoicing. It's something I would never have done had I not personally watched John Barros. If you want to evangelize, find an evangelist and shadow them for a while. Follow them as they follow Christ.

Gear

The second thing firefighters have that equips them for their job is fire equipment. Helmet, fireproof jacket, oxygen mask, boots, and an axe are all pieces of the fireman's "armor." Christians have armor, the full armor of God; we looked at each piece in the last chapter. What would you think of a fireman who ran into a burning building without his gear? I'm sure his commander wouldn't be happy with him. He not only wouldn't be very effective at his task, but he would very likely suffer injury himself. I think the same would apply to a Christian who runs into evangelism without the full armor of God. Don't forget your gear. So many Christians have more than enough gear; that is, they know the Word, they know where things are in the Bible, they know how to explain the gospel to someone, but they sadly never use it.

They're like a martial arts master of long ago who was given a gift of a rare samurai sword. Handcrafted by a legendary blacksmith, it was the sharpest in the land. The sword was placed in a glass case in the master's living room. One day a band of robbers broke down the front door as the master sipped tea. When the robbers saw the sword in the case behind the master, they hesitated, realizing they had made a huge mistake. The master then grabbed a toothpick, waved it around and ran toward the robbers. The robbers laughed, and then they killed him.

Christians have the sword of the Spirit, yet they often reach for the toothpick of scientific arguments, moral claims, intellectual answers, and every other inferior method of reasoning toward the gospel. There will never be anything stronger than God's Word. I am not saying that additional forms of information other than the Bible are worthless, but if you are not using the Bible as your primary weapon of attack and defense as you proclaim the gospel, you are fighting foolishly. Put down the toothpick; your witnessing will be much more efficient when you use the sword of the Spirit, which is the Word of God.

Experience

Imagine your home is burning. You are frantic because your child is inside, trapped in a room. Two firemen stand at the door—one is about to enter to find your child; the other is needed to battle the blaze. Firefighter number one is eighteen years old, fresh out of the academy. His uniform is spotless; he has a shiny helmet, polished boots, and a freshly shaved face. He is smiling weakly, but you can't tell if he's trying to be nice, or just nervous. Young and handsome, he is a candidate for the annual firehouse calendar.

Firefighter number two is about ten years older. His face is weathered. There is a large scar on his chin. His helmet is dented, and his jacket is pretty worn; it's about time for a new one. The ax in his hand is so beat, it looks like he's chopped down a forest. There is no smile on his face; he's as calm and focused as can be. He's thinking through the room layout and formulating his plan to locate the child and get out. He's standing next to the rookie to train him what to do. Which one of these guys do you want to go in after your child? Of course, you want the guy with the most experience.

Is it any wonder that a man like John MacArthur can explain the gospel better than you? He's been doing it for years, studying the Bible on weekdays and preaching every Sunday. Ray Comfort has been open-air preaching since he was twenty-four. He preached to crowds in New Zealand daily for many years, answering skeptics and hecklers on a regular basis. Do you think these men were perfectly clear and confident in their gospel presentation, able to answer any question and handle any objection when they began preaching? I doubt it. Experience is so valuable. How do you gain experience in evangelism? You evangelize, and then you do it again, and again and again.

The Case for Evangelizing Strangers

I've heard people say, "I only witness to people I know." That's great for your friends, but unless you know a lot of individuals, your evangelism will be limited. Two years from now, you can be at the same level of evangelism expertise you currently hold, or you can have two years of experience behind you. If you make an effort to evangelize strangers (and admittedly some are stranger than others), you will gain valuable experience. That experience will make a big difference during conversations with friends and family. And keep in mind that, from God's perspective, there are no strangers; only people He created who need to hear the gospel.

I find I love talking to strangers, which is rather odd because I was always a quiet, reserved person, more on the shy side. Even during my days of BMX stardom, when I was on the cover of magazines, I was not the superstar type. I just rode my bike and kept to myself. I have never been the kind of person who greets strangers or makes eye contact for more than a second with people I don't know. In other words, I'm normal. For the majority of my life, I was indifferent toward others. I was not hateful, but I just didn't care. I might have given to the needy once in a while and I never mocked the less fortunate. I was just self-centered, not concerned for others. When God saved me, that began to change. I did not change overnight, but over time my focus started to turn from myself toward the lost and I began to see the greatest need of the people around me: salvation from hell through Jesus Christ.

The gospel is the best news on the planet, and God has given us the privilege of sharing it with others. Stepping out of my comfort zone and learning to talk about Christ with people I don't know has been the joy of my life. God has changed my attitude toward the lost in ways I would have never imagined. I care about people and where they will spend eternity. I get grumpy when I haven't witnessed for a while (just ask my wife). The only explanation I can think of is that God has changed me, just as He changes and sanctifies every believer: *"I will give you a new heart and put a new spirit within you; and I will remove the heart of stone from your flesh and give you a heart of flesh"* (Ezekiel 36:26).

A Stranger No More

A funny thing happens when you talk to strangers; after a few minutes, they stop being strangers. Once you get their name and give them yours, you are no longer strangers. Yesterday I approached two men on a college campus and handed them both gospel tracts in the form of million-dollar bills. One of them asked what it was for. I told him it was a million-dollar bill with the million-dollar question on the back. He smiled and asked what the million-dollar question was, so I said to him, "What do you think happens after you die?" He said, "That's a good question." It turns out he came from Iran four years ago. He told me his name and that he was a Buddhist who used to be a Muslim. His friend was a Muslim from the Philippines who used to be Catholic. I told them I was a Christian from California, so I'm boring compared to them. I asked the Iranian, "Isn't it great that we can all have different beliefs in this country, talk about them openly, and no one's going to die?" He got serious and said, "Yes, it is."

Later in the conversation, he talked about the strictness of Islam and how horrible some men can be. He told me he liked

Buddhism because it makes sense to him, and he's more of a free spirit. I listened and just let him talk. He seemed like a nice guy, glad to be in America, enjoying his newfound freedom in a place where he is not obligated to believe in a particular religion. He then asked the perfect question. Referring to his friend, the former Catholic (who had left the conversation), he said, "I've always wanted to know the difference between Catholics and Christians. Can you tell me?" What would you have said to him? I bet many of you would do what I did; I talked about justification by faith alone vs. attempting to work your way to heaven. If you can explain that, you are more than ready to evangelize the lost.

He listened as I explained the difference. When I was done, he thanked me. He told me about his atheist dad, still in Iran, and his mom, a divorced Muslim living with him here in California. I asked him if I could explain the main message of Christianity to him (even though I had already covered most of it). He said yes. I told him that the easiest way for me to do that is to ask him some questions, and as he answers the message will be made clear. I then took him through the Good Person Test. He followed along, admitting his sin at every point (that he was a liar, thief, etc.). In the end, he understood. This Muslim-turned-Buddhist, for the first time in his life, heard the gospel and was thankful for the explanation. His class was starting, so he had to go. I gave him a business card with information about my church and invited him to come. I told him about the college group and the Friday night meetings. He was interested and thankful. We shook hands and off he went.

Will I see him at my church? I don't know. Will I see him in heaven? I hope so. The seed has been planted; now it's in

God's hands. The conversation was not dramatic, and it was not difficult. Most of my gospel encounters are like this, no drama. We have this notion that everyone hates the name of Jesus and at the first mention of Him we will be spit on or worse. In most of America, that is just not true. Many do hate our Lord, but many do not.

So take a risk. The next time you see a stranger walking toward you, how can you know if the person is saved or not? There's one way to find out. Hand the person a tract and ask the million-dollar question. My encounter with the Buddhist from Iran is not unique; many people will be happy to get into a spiritual conversation if you instigate it. One of the reasons I evangelize in places with many people (the beach, college campuses, etc.) is that there are more people to talk to. Some people may ignore me and throw away my tracts, but many will take them. It may feel embarrassing to offer someone a tract that gets rejected, but if you keep offering it, someone will take it. Before you know it, you'll be talking to someone about Jesus, the most important name they will ever hear.

First Steps

If you haven't yet given public evangelism a try, I suggest the following steps or stepping-stones. For those who would rather not dive into evangelism like I did (I open-air preached on Hollywood Blvd. before ever having a one-to-one witnessing conversation), here's a typical progression.

1. **Tract drop:** Leave gospel tracts in places where people can find them. On bulletin boards, in laundromats, inside

magazines in waiting rooms, tucked inside cases of beer at grocery stores, etc. Be creative, just don't do anything illegal. It is not illegal to leave tracts.

2. **Tracting:** Personally hand gospel tracts to people. Crowded places work best. Just smile as you hand them out and say, "This is for you," or, "Here you go." When people do not take them, don't be discouraged; just give one to the next person. You don't even need to say anything, just hand them out, and you'll get the gospel into the hands and minds of many.

3. **One-to-one witnessing:** Use gospel tracts as a way to begin conversations with people. While handing one out, ask, "Did you get one of these?" You'll get the reply, "What is it?" You can say, "It's about God and heaven. Do you ever think about that kind of stuff?" At that point, they may dismiss themselves, or they may stop to talk. If they do not stop, try it again. If the next person does not stop, do it again until someone stops. Someone will. I have never handed out tracts in this way without someone stopping to talk.

If you can make one-to-one witnessing a regular part of your life, God will use you for great things. What could be better than communicating the gospel to unbelievers and leading people to Christ? For the Christian, it is one of the most fulfilling things you can ever do. Your Christian experience can be so much more than just going to church and trying not to sin. Step out in faith, and with the Lord's help you can witness to strangers.

Big Step

Occasionally I talk to men who have been witnessing for years who now want to try open-air preaching. For those who are ready to get on the box, I don't know any shortcuts. If you are already preaching in a church, you are more than ready. Prepare a five-minute gospel message and give it a go. Make sure to cover the law, sin, judgment, hell, God's mercy, the cross, the resurrection, repentance, and faith. I often try to engage people with questions as I preach, with the goal of taking them through the Good Person Test while others listen in. Sometimes I'll read and explain a passage that is loaded with the gospel, such as Ephesians 2:8–10, Colossians 1:13–18, John 3, etc. Remember you are talking to non-church people, so be careful not to use language that only Christians understand (like "washed in the blood").

As mentioned in chapter 1, in recent years I've taken up sketchboard evangelism, a technique of painting your way through a gospel message. It requires some basic art training and practice, but it can be very useful in drawing a crowd. I am not an artist by any stretch of the imagination, but I was able to learn the sketchboard technique. Many good open-air preachers got their start with sketchboard evangelism; it's a great way to get comfortable with public speaking. The ministry of Open Air Campaigners provides training and guidance, as well as messages for you to preach. For more information on this unique form of evangelism, visit the OAC website.[15]

Friendship Evangelism

"Friendship evangelism" is a method of witnessing where Christians make friends in order to evangelize to them. The concept is, if unbelievers get to know you, they will see your Christian character and want whatever it is you have that makes you a good person.

15 Open Air Campaigners can be found at oacusa.org.

The ideal opportunity arrives when the unbeliever asks something along the lines of, "So, why are you such a loving, caring, kind, giving, forgiving individual?" At this point, the Christian can take the opportunity to swoop in and preach the gospel. Since the unbeliever now has the gospel information, as well as the character evidence to back up the message, the gospel is sure to be received. Those who practice this tactic often cite the erroneous saying supposedly attributed to Francis of Assisi, "Preach the gospel at all times, and if necessary, use words."

There are so many problems with this tactic. Friendship evangelism begins with the assumption that we need to earn the right to preach the gospel, and that is just not true. Remember the Great Commission? *"All authority has been given to Me in heaven and on earth. Go therefore and make disciples"* (Matthew 28:18,19). Jesus said He has "all authority." He was given authority from the Father, and with that authority, He authorized and commanded us to go. We do not need permission; we just need to obey. There is no need to "earn the right" by being a good friend or doing good works before you can talk about Jesus, the only one who can grant everlasting life. You should be doing good works already, as a result of the Spirit living in you. We should never be afraid to talk about Christ with our unbelieving friends or strangers.

Also, the supposed call to "preach the gospel at all times, and if necessary, use words," makes absolutely no sense when you think of the biblical definition of the gospel. Remember, it's the death and resurrection of Jesus Christ. How are we to preach that without words—by miming it? In order to preach the gospel you must use words, as Romans 10:14 tells us: *"How will they hear without a preacher?"*

I understand it's good to be tactful, but if you think that waiting six months or a year to "come out" as a Christian is a good idea, you are mistaken. The disciples never hid their identity; they wanted everyone to know they were of Christ. If you are afraid that your friends will reject you once you start talking about Jesus, your issue isn't evangelism tactics, it's your fear of man. This problem is not new; it's been around since Jesus walked the earth: *"Nevertheless many even of the rulers believed in Him, but because of the Pharisees they were not confessing Him, for fear that they would be put out of the synagogue; for they loved the approval of men rather than the approval of God"* (John 12:42,43). If you have been suppressing your desire to witness to your friends as a result of fear, repent. For all you know, one of them is ripe for harvest.

Early in my Christian walk, I learned this firsthand. I went on a work-related trip to Africa for two weeks. One of the guys on the trip (let's call him "Eric") was a heavy partier, regularly drinking and talking about his sexual escapades with women. I wrote him off as a fool. We had meals together each day and traveled side by side. We talked about trivial things, everything except the gospel. The trip went well; we got along fine. I kept my mouth shut about Christ and thankfully Eric didn't overdose on anything. At the end of the trip, our group of ten had our last meal together. One of the guys in the group who knew me a little better asked, "Eddie, are you glad to be getting back to your church?" At that, Eric blurted out, "You're a Christian? Why didn't you tell me?!!! I don't know any Christians, and I've wanted to talk to someone about getting right with God!" He was so upset, and I felt about as big as maggot larvae.

I could have been discipling Eric for two weeks, but instead, I chose to tiptoe around the unbelievers in fear. After that meal, I was too embarrassed to talk with Eric, and he probably didn't think very highly of me, the so-called Christian who never talks about Jesus. Don't make that same mistake, friend; be known as a Christian. Talk about Christ with the people around you.

Another problem with "friendship evangelism" is the fact that Christians are not the only ones doing good works. Mormons, Catholics, humanitarians, and Boy Scouts all do good works. Good works do not communicate the gospel; only your mouth does that. Did you know Mormons are actively involved in good works as a means of spreading their message? I've had Mormon missionaries offer to wash my car. The lazy side of me wanted to let them, but I rejected the offer because I would never want my neighbors to see Mormons at my house and associate me with them. That is part of their tactic—they wash your car, then go to your neighbor and say, "Yeah, we know Eddie, we were just over at his house..."

I believe we should be involved in biblical friendship evangelism. Make friends, preach the gospel to them, and continue being a good friend. If they reject Christ, pray for them and continue being a friend, as long as it does not cause you to compromise. I have friends who are Muslim, homosexual, atheist, and many other brands of non-Christian. We are not friends in the sense of sharing common goals and beliefs, but we are much more than acquaintances. I genuinely care for them. Whether it's a BMX memory or a shared interest in filmmaking, I have much in common with many unbelievers. We talk, sometimes laugh and spend time together, but I do not compromise on the things of God. For example, I will not go to a strip bar to build a relationship with someone. If I'm in a group of old friends and someone makes a crude comment that causes everyone to laugh, I don't join in. That can be awkward, being the only one who isn't laughing at a crude joke, but it's one small way to follow Christ in the midst of unbelievers. If your friends have heard the gospel from you already, your conduct is a great reminder that they need to get right with God.

Press On

Whether we attempt to evangelize friends, acquaintances, or strangers, we must not become discouraged when we don't see immediate results. Our job is to preach the gospel, while God is the one who saves. Paul modeled this throughout his ministry. He communicated the gospel and left the results to God. Sometimes people rejected and sometimes they accepted what he had to say. When Paul preached his famous message in the Areopagus, people reacted in different ways. After he finished explaining the gospel, the Bible tells us, *"When they heard of the resurrection of the dead, some began to sneer, but others said, 'We shall hear you again concerning this.' So Paul went out of their midst. But some men joined him and believed, among whom also were Dionysius the Areopagite and a woman named Damaris and others with them"* (Acts 17:32–34). When you read that, do you focus on the men who sneered or those who joined him and believed? There will always be mockers, but we shouldn't let that discourage us.

Paul left the Areopagus and continued preaching the gospel, and the results continued to vary.

When Silas and Timothy came down from Macedonia, Paul begin devoting himself completely to the word, solemnly testifying to the Jews that Jesus was the Christ. But when they resisted and blasphemed, he shook out his garments and said to them, "Your blood be on your own heads! I am clean. From now on I will go to the Gentiles." Then he left there and went to the house of a man named Titius Justus, a worshiper of God, whose house was next to the synagogue. Crispus, the leader of the synagogue, believed in the Lord with all his household, and many of the Corinthians when they heard were believing and being baptized. (Acts 18:5–8)

Isn't it interesting that one group resisted and blasphemed, while another group believed and were baptized? This is normal—some reject while others accept. This is why it's so important to press on. Serving Christ through evangelism is not a hobby; it shouldn't be something we do for a while and give up. Personal evangelism shouldn't be an event that happened long ago, perhaps on a short-term mission trip. We all go through various seasons of life as believers, but there's no reason to think it's okay to leave evangelism behind.

The Big Picture

Evangelism is one aspect of our faith as Christians. It is not more important or less important than any other part; we should be following Christ in every area He asks us to. Sometimes people who are active in evangelism are weak in other areas, like fellowship. I've met evangelists who have no patience for believers who do not share their zeal for the lost. I've seen guys become bitter toward fellow believers because they will not join the street witnessing team. This attitude can evolve into a hardness toward fellowship which can result in a Lone Ranger mentality. That attitude misses the big picture. Every Christian is growing; we are all at different places in our walk. We all need each other to grow, and the local church is where that happens: *"But now God has placed the members, each one of them, in the body, just as He desired. If they were all one member, where would the body be? But now there are many members, but one body. And the eye cannot say to the hand, 'I have no need of you'; or again the head to the feet, 'I have no need of you'"* (1 Corinthians 12:18–21).

Church life is an important part of our growth, as is obedience to the Word. I've met Christians who are proud of their evangelism skills, but blind to their arrogance or impatience. Each of us must allow the Word to change us, not only in the area of evangelism, but in every area of our lives. James 1:22 warns us, *"Prove yourselves doers of the word, and not merely hearers who delude themselves."* Evangelism is one piece of the picture; our walk with Christ is the big picture. As we do His will by obeying His Word, He will use us as He wishes.

Step Out

As I draw to a close, I think of how the Holy Spirit has used my evangelism encounters to mold me in many ways. My compassion for the lost has grown with each rejection of Christ. My joy for the Lord has increased over the years as I've watched friends and family members repent and believe. I've led evangelism classes and street teams, and years later listened to those I taught as they led others to Christ. Jesus saves, and He blesses us with joy as we labor with Him. One of the greatest benefits for me concerning evangelism has been a clear conscience. Knowing that I am obedient to Christ's command to fulfill the Great Commission is a blessing beyond words. I understand what Paul meant when he explained his preaching to Felix in Acts 24: *"having a hope in God, which these men cherish themselves, that there shall certainly be a resurrection of both the righteous and the wicked. In view of this, I also do my best to maintain always a blameless conscience both before God and before men"* (Acts 24:15,16).

Who do you want to witness to? Is your conscience prodding you to explain the gospel to someone? If so, don't push it aside. Step out in faith, follow Christ, and let Him make you into a faithful fisher of men (and women). May God bless you as you take the gospel to the people He has placed in your life.

QUESTIONS FOR REFLECTION

1. What three practical things can help you become better at evangelism? _____

2. What is one of the advantages of evangelizing strangers? What are other reasons we should do so? _____

3. How would you describe the difference between a works-based religion and Christianity? _____

4. What is the million-dollar question, and how is it used with the million-dollar tract? _____

_____

5. Is it necessary to "earn the right" to explain the gospel to someone? Why or why not? _____

_____

6. Why is it a bad idea to conceal your identity as a believer?

_____

_____

7. When Paul preached the gospel, did he become discouraged when people rejected his message? Why not? _____

_____

_____

8. In Acts 24:15,16, Paul speaks of his clear conscience. Why was his conscience clear? _____

_____

_____

9. Is there someone in your life who you should witness to? Who? Ask God to help you witness to them. _____

_____

_____

WATCH THIS! //

- "Only one life, 'twill soon be past; only what's done for Christ will last."—C.T. Studd
- Go to eddieroman.com and click Watch on the top menu.
- Watch the video labeled "It Will Cost You Everything."

PRAYER POINT //

- Ask God to make evangelism a regular part of your Christian walk.

CONCLUSION

In chapter 1, I shared the embarrassing personal story of my encounter with Rave Girl. Looking back, it's silly how a teenager with an attitude shut me down and took me out of the Great Commission for years. It was a weird chapter of my life, yet I know it was a very real hindrance to my evangelism at the time. As you've read this book, maybe you've thought about your own evangelism attempts—the good, the bad, and the ugly. I want to encourage you to press on. Learning to witness is a process, not a one-time event. This can be a hard concept to grasp in America, land of fast food, fast entertainment, and fast everything else. Whatever it is, we usually want it now. So I want to encourage you to be patient with yourself. You probably will not become a skilled evangelist in one week. Confidence in apologetics may take time. I spent a good three years learning about presuppositional apologetics before I was comfortable using it with unbelievers on the street. Getting to a place where I'm comfortable discussing the Trinity took a while for me as well.

In Ray Comfort's autobiography, *Out of the Comfort Zone*, he describes himself in the early days before he began public evangelism. Ray is currently the most famous street evangelist in the world, but back then he was terrified to talk to people! He remembers being on a city bus, surrounded by people, wanting to share the gospel, yet too afraid to speak. What made the difference? Mainly thinking about the fate of the lost; remembering that he's only risking embarrassment, while they're facing eternity in hell is what gave him the courage to start speaking. From there, time had a lot to do with how well he did.

So give yourself time. Don't allow Satan or anyone else to discourage you as you embark on a lifelong outreach to the lost. Talk about Christ at the grocery store, at school, and anywhere else you find unbelievers. They're usually all around us so it shouldn't be a problem. When you mess up a witnessing encounter, humbly ask the Lord to help you do better the next time and move on. If you are not confident with your gospel presentation, practice. Review chapters 2 and 3. If you know the gospel, you should be able to communicate it in a simple way.

Know Your Enemy

Knowing the Bible should be a top priority. That being said, it's also good to learn all you can about the cults and false religions in your area. Books on apologetics and theology can be a huge help to your evangelism encounters. In his classic book *The Art of War*, Sun Tzu said, "If you know your enemies and know yourself, you will not be put at risk even in a hundred battles." If the advancement of the gospel is considered a win, then I would agree, we can win many battles, but we need to understand the enemy. Satan is a deceiver, so the more we know his schemes by reading Scripture, the better we can fight against him and the many cults and false religions he empowers.

The risks associated with evangelism are real, but they are also worth it. Feelings of embarrassment, awkwardness, and fear pass with time and experience. Learning to witness is like riding a bike; it's hard at first, but the more you practice, the more natural it becomes.

All for Christ

Christian, the day is coming quickly when you will be in heaven. The chance to witness to the people around you will be gone. Moses prayed to the Lord, *"Teach us to number our days, that we may present to You a heart of wisdom"* (Psalm 90:12). Our days are numbered, and sadly, so are the days of the lost around us. As you go through your day, ask yourself, "In what way am I living for Christ? In what way am I using my time wisely for the Lord? Take the opportunity to glorify Christ through evangelism now, while you have the opportunity. You will not regret it.

> Our days are numbered, and sadly, so are the days of the lost around us.

"Go therefore and make disciples of all the nations, baptizing them in the name of the Father and the Son and the Holy Spirit, teaching them to observe all that I commanded you; and lo, I am with you always, even to the end of the age."

(Matthew 28:19,20)

SUGGESTED RESOURCES

Websites

- livingwaters.com
  —The best evangelism website on the planet. Home of Ray Comfort and the million-dollar gospel tract.
- aomin.org
  —The apologetics of James White. James has formally debated Muslims, atheists, Catholics, and representatives from most of the major religious movements. His writings and online debates are a wealth of apologetics information from a Reformed perspective.
- answersingenesis.org
  —A biblical perspective on the creation/evolution debate.
- creationtoday.org
  —Apologetics dealing with evolution.
- proofthatgodexists.org
  —Presuppositional apologetics by Sye Ten Bruggencate.
- eddieroman.com
  —Evangelism resources, encouragement, and instruction.

Books

- *The Forgotten Trinity* by James White
  —The Trinity, thoroughly explained.

- *Oneness Pentecostals & the Trinity* by Gregory Boyd
  —A thorough refutation of modalism.
- *From Buddha to Jesus* by Steve Cioccolanti
  —Insight on reaching Buddhists for Christ.
- *Out of the Comfort Zone* by Ray Comfort
  —The encouraging testimony of Ray Comfort's evangelism journey.
- *The Way of the Master* by Ray Comfort
  —A wonderful resource on evangelism.

ABOUT THE AUTHOR

Eddie Roman is the producer/director of the *Way of the Master* television program, a show that teaches Christians how to evangelize. Eddie has created programming for many Christian ministries including The Billy Graham Association, Samaritan's Purse, and Harvest: Greg Laurie. He previously served as a missionary photographer/videographer, working in Sudan, Indonesia, Burma, Pakistan, and many other third-world countries. Eddie began as a professional BMX Freestyle rider, competing and performing in stunt demonstrations around the world, prior to working in action sports, with his programming appearing on Fox Sports Network, ESPN, and MTV.

Early in his Christian walk, Eddie taught Bible studies and went on mission trips, but did not share his faith. After many years of fear and complacency, he became involved in evangelism, and God dramatically changed his life.

Eddie leads the evangelism ministry at Faith Bible Church in Temecula, California. He lives with his wife, Carri, and their sons, Jesse, Matthew, Daniel, and Christopher.

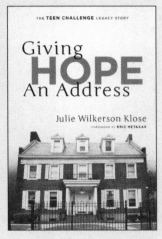

RESTORED AND FORGIVEN
Ray & Vi Donovan

Ray and Vi Donovan were awoken in the early hours of the morning to the horrific news that their two sons had been brutally attacked by a gang. One of their sons, Christopher, later died from his injuries. Through their faith in God and the Restorative Justice system, Ray and Vi transformed their anger into a force for good. In this powerful and moving testimony, the Donavans explain how they have forgiven the boys that senselessly murdered their son.

Ray and Vi have become prolific campaigners for restorative justice, giving talks in prisons, schools, probation services, YOTs, and youth clubs across the UK.

www.chrisdonovantrust.org

ISBN: 978-1-61036-970-1

BEAUTY FROM ASHES
Donna Sparks

In a transparent and powerful manner, the author reveals how the Lord took her from the ashes of a life devastated by failed relationships and destructive behavior to bring her into a beautiful and powerful relationship with Him. The author encourages others to allow the Lord to do the same for them.

Donna Sparks is an Assemblies of God evangelist who travels widely to speak at women's conferences and retreats. She lives in Tennessee.

www.story-of-grace.com

www.facebook.com/
donnasparksministries/

https://www.facebook.com/
AuthorDonnaSparks/

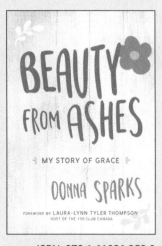

ISBN: 978-1-61036-252-8

ALL THE WILD PEARLS
Heather DeJesus Yates

Every pearl has a story to tell. Join lawyer, speaker and author Heather DeJesus Yates as she creatively guides our generation through the transformational hope of the Gospel using both her own redemptive stories and those of an unlikely companion...a wild oyster.

Heather DeJesus Yates is a wife, mama, business owner, speaker, blogger, occasional lawyer and legislative advocate, and author. Out of a passion to see women walk in freedom from shame, Heather woos women into God's wide love through her disarmingly real-life stories, balanced with Gospel-centered hope.

Facebook: @amotherofthousands
Instagram: @amotherofthousands
Pinterest: @amotherofthousands.
www.facebook.com/amotherofthousands
www.amotherofthousands.com

ISBN: 978-1-61036-991-6

BRIDGE
LOGOS

FINDING JOY WHEN LIFE IS OUT OF FOCUS

Angela Donadio

We all walk through seasons when joy plays an unwelcome game of hide and seek. This in-depth, verse by verse study will help you choose contentment regardless of circumstance, transform faulty thought patterns through the truth of God's Word, and persevere when life is unravelling. Filled with personal testimony and encouragement, this would be an ideal companion for groups or personal study.

Angela Donadio is an international speaker, recording artist, and advocate for deprived pastors' wives and children in Africa.

www.angeladonadio.com

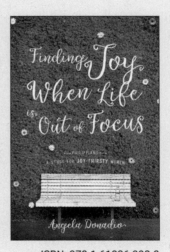

ISBN: 978-1-61036-993-0

BRIDGE
LOGOS